STUDY GUIDE

Fundamentals of

Management

STUDY GUIDE
JAMES V. DUPREE
Grove City College

Fundamentals of
Management
THIRD EDITION

ESSENTIAL CONCEPTS AND APPLICATIONS

STEPHEN P. ROBBINS
DAVID A. DECENZO

Prentice
Hall

Upper Saddle River, New Jersey 07458

Acquisitions editor: Melissa Steffens
Associate editor: Jessica Sabloff
Production editor: Theresa Festa
Manufacturer: Daamen, Inc.

ISBN 0-13-087450-7

10 9 8 7 6 5 4 3 2 1

Contents

PART 1 - INTRODUCTION
CHAPTER 1 - MANAGERS AND MANAGEMENT

LEARNING OUTCOMES
After reading this chapter, you should be able to:
1. Describe the difference between managers and operative employees.
2. Explain what is meant by the term *management*.
3. Differentiate between efficiency and effectiveness.
4. Describe the four primary processes of management.
5. Classify the three levels of managers, and identify the primary responsibility of each group.
6. Summarize the essential roles performed by managers.
7. Discuss whether the manager's job is generic.
8. Describe the four general skills necessary for becoming a successful manager.
9. Describe the value of studying management.
10. Identify the relevance of popular humanities and social science courses to management practices.

Use the Outline to Guide Your Note Taking from the Text

Considerations as you read

As you read and take notes, think about these questions; they will help you organize your study notes.
1. What characterizes an organization and how does this influence the job of the manager?
2. What can you learn from each of the theories of management that can help you be a more effective manager?
3. How does the manager's job differ by organizational level in terms of responsibilities, skills, and competencies?
4. What do other academic disciplines contribute to managers' understanding of their profession and practice?

I. WHO ARE MANAGERS, AND WHERE DO THEY WORK?
A. Introduction
    1. Managers work in an organization.
    2. An organization is
        a) An example

B. What Three Common Characteristics Do All Organizations Share?
    1. Every organization has
        a) See Exhibit 1-1.
        b) The distinct purpose of an organization is
    2. Second,
        a) It takes
    3. Third, all organizations develop
        a) Developing structure may include,
    4. Organization — an entity that has

C. How Are Managers Different from Operative Employees?
    1. Organizational members fit into two categories:
        a) Operatives
        b) Managers
    2. The distinction, managers

D. What Titles Do Managers Have in Organizations?
1. First-line managers are usually called
   a) They are responsible for
   b) In your college, the
2. Middle managers — management
   a) They manage
   b) They are responsible for
3. Top managers, like Wiin Wu are responsible for

II. WHAT IS MANAGEMENT, AND WHAT DO MANAGERS DO?
A. How Do We Define Management?
1. Managers, regardless of title, share several common elements.
2. Management — the process of
   a) Process in the definition represents
3. Effectiveness and efficiency deal with
   a) Efficiency —
   b) Effectiveness —
   c) See Exhibit 1-3.
4. Efficiency and effectiveness are interrelated.
   a) It's easier to be
   b) Good management is
   c) Organizations can be
   d) High efficiency is associated more typically with
5. Poor management is most often due to

B. What Are the Management Processes?
1. Henri Fayol defined the management process in terms of five management functions.
   a) They
   b) In the mid-1950s, two professors
2. The most popular textbooks organize around
   a) See Exhibit 1-4.
   b) These processes are interrelated and interdependent.
3. Planning
4. Organizing
5. Leading
   a) Managers
6. Controlling
   a) To ensure that
   b) Actual performance must be
   c) Any significant deviations
   d) The monitoring, comparing, and correcting is
7. The process approach is
   a) Fayol's original applications represented
8. Henry Mintzberg

C. What Are Management Roles?
1. Henry Mintzberg undertook a careful study of five chief executives at work.
   a) Managers engaged in
   b) There was little
   c) Half of these managers' activities
2. His categorization scheme — Mintzberg's managerial roles.

3. Mintzberg concluded that managers perform ten different but highly interrelated roles.
    a) These ten roles are shown in Exhibit 1-5.
    b) They are grouped under three primary headings.

D. Is the Manager's Job Universal?
1. Level in the Organization.
    a) The differences are of
    b) As managers move up, they
    c) The amount of time managers give to each activity is
    d) The content of the managerial activities
2. Profit v. Not-for-Profit.
    a) The manager's job is mostly
    b) All managers,
    c) The most important is
    d) There is no
    e) Making a profit for the not-for-profit organizations is
    f) The two are far more alike than they are different.
3. Size of Organization.
    a) Definition of small business and the part it plays in our society.
    b) Small business —
    c) Statistics on small business.
    d) Managing a small business is different from that of managing a large one.
    e) We see differences in degree and emphasis, but not in activities.
4. Management Concepts and National Borders.
    a) Studies do not generally
    b) Most of the concepts we will be discussing in future chapters primarily apply to
5. Making Decisions and Dealing with Change.
    a) Managers make decisions, and managers are agents of change.
    b) Successful managers acknowledge

E. What Skills and Competencies Do Successful Managers Possess?
1. In the 1970s, management researcher Robert L. Katz, found
2. Management skills
    a) Two perspectives — general skills and the specific skills.
3. General Skills.
    a) Conceptual skills refer to
    b) Interpersonal skills encompass
    c) Technical skills are abilities to
    d) Political skills are related to
4. Specific Skills.
    a) Research has also identified six sets of behaviors that explain a little bit more than 50 percent of a manager's effectiveness.
5. Management Competencies.
    a) The most recent approach to defining the manager's job.
    b) These are defined as a cluster of
    c) One of the most comprehensive competency studies is out of the United Kingdom.
    d) The MCI standards are attracting global interest.

III. HOW MUCH IMPORTANCE DOES THE MARKETPLACE PUT ON MANAGERS?
A. Introduction
1. Good managers can turn straw to gold.

2. Managers tend to be more highly paid than operatives.
   a) As a manager's authority and responsibility expand, so typically does
   b) Large toy-manufacturing firms such as Mattel and Fisher Price
3. However, not all managers make
4. What could you expect to earn as a manager?
   a) It depends on
   b) Most first-line supervisors earn between
   c) Middle managers often start near
   d) Senior managers in large corporations can earn
   e) In 1998, the average cash compensation (salary plus annual bonus) for 483 of the top two executives at the 392 largest publicly held U.S. corporations was well over

IV. WHY STUDY MANAGEMENT?
A. Reasons
1. We all have a vested interest in improving the way organizations are managed.
   a) We interact with them every day of our lives.
   b) Those that are poorly managed often find
2. The reality that, once you graduate from college and begin your career, you will either
   a) An understanding of the management process is
   b) You will almost certainly work
   c) You needn't aspire to be a manager to gain something valuable from
3. Management embodies

V. HOW DOES MANAGEMENT RELATE TO OTHER DISCIPLINES?
A. Introduction
1. College courses frequently appear to be independent bodies of knowledge.
2. There is typically a lack of
3. A number of management educators have begun to recognize
4. We've integrated topics around
5. The big picture is often lost when management concepts are studied in isolation.

B. What Can Students of Management Gain from Humanities and Social Science Courses?
1. Anthropology.
   a) The study of
   b) Anthropologists' work
2. Economics.
   a) Concerned with the
3. Philosophy.
   a) Philosophy courses inquire into
   b) Ethical concerns go directly to
4. Political Science.
   a) It studies
   b) Specific topics of concern include
   c) Capitalism is
   d) The economies based on socialistic concepts are
   e) Management is affected by a
5. Psychology.
   a) The science that seeks to
   b) Psychologists study and attempt to understand
   c) Psychology courses are also relevant to managers in terms of

6. Sociology.
    a) Sociology studies people in relation to
    b) Sociologists investigate how

REVIEW QUESTIONS

1. How does Wiin Wu's experience with Macronix demonstrate the functions and roles of management?
   Answer – Pages 2-3

2. What is an organization? What characteristics are common to all organizations?
   Answer – Page 3

3. Describe the differences between non-management employees (operatives) and managers.
   Answer – Pages 3-4

4. Define management.
   Answer – Page 5

5. Are all effective organizations also efficient? What is the difference?
   Answer – Page 5

6. Name and explain the four common management activities of the process approach to management.
   Answer – Pages 6-8

7. Contrast the four elements of the process approach to management with Henry Mintzberg's ten roles.
   Answer – Page 8 and Exhibit 1.5

8. How is the manager's job different in a non-profit from his/her job in a for profit firm?
   Answer – Page 10

9. How does the size of an organization impact the manager's job?
   Answer – Pages 11-12

10. Robert L. Katz identified a set of general skills and specific skills that affect managerial effectiveness. Identify and explain both sets and the specific skills within them.
    Answer – Pages 13-15

11. What is the MCI and its implications for management?
    Answer – Pages 14-15

12. Review the compensation and responsibilities of managers based on their level within a firm.
    Answer – Pages 16-18

13. How do the disciplines of anthropology, economics, philosophy, political science, psychology, and sociology contribute to understanding and the practice of management?
    Answer – Pages 18-20

STUDY QUIZ
Multiple Choice Questions

1. Buzz is working on job descriptions, company policies, and who to assign to what project teams. His efforts represent which common characteristic of an organization?
   - a) Purpose
   - b) People
   - c) Structure None of these

2. Wiin Wu in Macronix is an example of a/an:
   - a) first-line manager.
   - b) middle manager.
   - c) top manager.
   - d) operative.

3. Which of the following is true about the relationship of effectiveness and efficiency?
   - a) They are independent variables and not interrelated.
   - b) It is not enough to be efficient; an organization must also be effective.
   - c) Organizations cannot be effective and efficient at the same time.
   - d) Poor management is largely the result of ineffectiveness due to gross inefficiency.

4. _____ describes the management process.
   - a) The systematic arrangement of people brought together to accomplish some specific purpose
   - b) The performance of a job or task by doing it on an individual basis
   - c) The process of getting things done, through and with others,
   - d) None of these

5. If Jo is working on the goals and purpose of her work unit, she is performing the _____ component of the management process.
   - a) planning
   - b) organizing
   - c) leading
   - d) controlling

6. What effect does organizational level have on the manager's job?
   - a) None, all managers perform the same functions to the same degree regardless of level.
   - b) It changes the content of the manager's activities.
   - c) A great deal, there are almost no commonalities in function among first-line, middle, and top managers.
   - d) A little in that it affects only management components, i.e., first-line managers control more than top managers, top managers plan less than middle managers, etc.

7. Small businesses, of over 500 employees,
   - a) create nearly 2 million jobs annually.
   - b) have a net loss of 40% of their workforce over the last year.
   - c) account for 47 percent of all non-farm business in the United States.
   - d) employ nearly 90% of the workforce.

8. All managers, regardless of level in an organization or the size of the organization:
   a) are entrepreneurs and focus on allocating resources.
   b) share few if any commonalities in role, function, or skills.
   c) spend the same amount of time on their management functions.
   d) make decisions and function as change agents.

9. The four critical general management skills for manager effectiveness, according to Katz, include:
   a) controlling.
   b) handling information.
   c) technical skills.
   d) hiring.

10. _____ is when managers take responsibility for their decisions, ensure that subordinates properly use their decision-making skills, and is a specific skill that managers need to be effective.
    a) Strategic problem solving
    b) Handling information
    c) Controlling
    d) Organizing and coordinating

11. The Management Charter Initiative:
    a) has developed standards for first-line and middle manager effectiveness.
    b) is developing standards for middle manager effectiveness.
    c) is based on comprehensive studies in the United Kingdom.
    d) includes all of these.

12. Middle manager compensation often starts at _____ and is capped at:
    a) $30,000; $50,000
    b) $65,000; $100,000
    c) $45,000; $120,000
    d) $140,000; $175,000

13. Your text offers several reasons why the study of management is important to all students, including:
    a) that all of us have a vested interest in how the companies we interact with are managed.
    b) its relationship with other disciplines in the humanities and social sciences.
    c) all of us are either managed or manage other people.
    d) all of these.

14. _____ is the social science that is concerned with the allocation and distribution of resources, and that helps managers view global competition.
    a) Economics
    b) Political Science
    c) Sociology
    d) Anthropology

15. The social science that helps managers study human relationships and helps and managers consider the impact of cultural diversity, globalization, family life, etc., on the conduct of business.
    a) Anthropology
    b) Sociology
    c) Political Science
    d) Psychology

True/False Questions

1. Wiin Wu's experience with Macronix demonstrates the truth that successful management is universal.

2. Tom's work with the goals for his company for the next year exemplifies the common organizational characteristic of purpose.

3. Willa supervises three other managers who are responsible for various areas of the assembly line in her plant. She reports to the plant manager. Willa is an example of a middle-manager.

4. Doing the right task, regardless of how well it is done, defines organizational effectiveness.

5. Han Chen is reassigning managers now that the big development push for the new product is over. He has placed some on another project team and given others individual assignments. Han's action demonstrates the planning element of the management process.

6. Mintzberg's research on management reversed the predominant view of management when he discovered that managers really are reflective thinkers and take a great deal of time making decisions.

7. Recent management innovation has enabled managers of non-profits to develop and use a universal, unambiguous, bottom-line- oriented measurement of performance.

8. Research shows that the entrepreneurial role is as important for managers in large companies as it is for managers in small businesses.

9. Management concepts do not appear to be generic, in that they must be modified as managers cross national boundaries due to cultural differences in workers.

10. When Nadia analyzes and diagnosis complex customer problems helping her sales staff to meet customer needs, she is using the general management skill, conceptual skills.

11. Motivating employees, strategic problem solving, and handling information are three examples of the specific skills that managers need to be effective.

12. First-line supervisors generally start at about $45,000 and go as high as $60,000 in the current job market.

13. It is important to study management because we all have to deal with various organizations, all of which are managed.

14. The social science discipline that helps managers understand the fundamental values, attitudes, and beliefs of people in different cultures and organizations is anthropology.

15. Political science is one of the few social sciences that really adds little of value to the management process and the understanding and practice of management.

Answers to Chapter 1 Study Quiz

Multiple Choice (Page - Answer)

1. c-3	6. b-8	11. d-14
2. c-4	7. a-11	12. c-16
3. b-5	8. d-12	13. d-17
4. c-6	9. c-13	14. a-19
5. a-6	10. a-14	15. b-20

True/False

1. F-2	6. F-8	11. T-14
2. T-3	7. F-10	12. F-16
3. T-4	8. F-11	13. T-17
4. T-5	9. T-12	14. T-18
5. F-6	10. T-13	15. F-19

HISTORY MODULE
THE HISTORICAL ROOTS OF CONTEMPORARY MANAGEMENT PRACTICES

Use the Outline to Guide Your Note Taking from the Text

Considerations as you read

As you read and take notes, think about these questions; they will help you organize your study notes.
1. What were three key events or concepts that shaped management theory in the pre-modern era.
2. Name the central contribution of each theorist in the classical school of management theory.
3. How did the human resources approach come into existence, and who were its major theorists?
4. What was the relationship or influence of the human relations movement on the human resources approach?
5. What gave rise to the quantitative approach to management theory? What made it more attractive than the current approaches to management?
6. Can you chart the key elements of process, contingency, and systems management theory?

I. INTRODUCTION
  A. The Purpose of This Module
    1. The knowledge of its history can
    2. It is an introduction to the origins of
    3. It shows that the evolution of management reflects

II. THE PRE-MODERN ERA
  A. Management Has Existed for Thousands of Years
    1. The Egyptian pyramids and the Great Wall of China
       a) These were projects of
    2. The pyramids
       a) The construction of a single pyramid
       b) Who
    3. Michelangelo
       a)
       b)
       c)
    4. Organized activities and managers have been
    5. It has been only in the past several hundred years

  B. What Was Adam Smith's Contribution to The Field of Management?
    1. Adam Smith's name is typically
       a) *The Wealth of Nations,*
       b) He used the pin-manufacturing industry for
       c) Working separately and independently, those ten workers
    2. He concluded that
    3. The wide popularity of job specialization is

  C. How Did The Industrial Revolution Influence Management Practices?
    1. Possibly the most important pre-twentieth-century influence on management.
       a) Begun in
       b) It crossed the Atlantic to
       c) Using machines made it

2. The advent of machine power,
   a) John D. Rockefeller
   b) Andrew Carnegie
3. A formal management theory

III. CLASSICAL CONTRIBUTIONS
A. The Roots of Modern Management
   1. Began with a group of practitioners
   2. The classical approach breaks into two subcategories.
      a)
      b)
B. What Contributions Did Frederick Taylor Make?
   1. 1911 was the year that
      a) Widely accepted, it
      b) The use of the scientific method
      c) Studies would establish Taylor as
   2. Frederick Taylor did most of his work at
      a) A mechanical engineer with a
      b) He spent more than
   3. Taylor sought to
   4. He defined four principles of management that would result in the prosperity of both management and workers.
      a) See Exhibit HM-1.
      b)
      c)
      d)
      e)
   5. The impact of Taylor's work cannot be overstated.
      a)
      b)
      c)
      d)
   6. In 1910, the Eastern Railroad
      a) An efficiency expert claimed
      b) This assertion became
      c) Then in 1911, Taylor published
   7. By 1914, Taylor's principles
   8. His method gave U.S. companies

C. Who Else, besides Taylor, Were Major Contributors to Scientific Management?
   1. Taylor's most prominent disciples
   2. Frank Gilbreth
      a) With wife Lillian
      b) The Gilbreths
      c) They were
   3. An associate of Taylor at Midvale and Bethlehem Steel
      a) Gantt sought to
      b) He devised
      c) He also introduced
      d) Gantt expanded
      e) He created

D. Why Did Scientific Management Receive So Much Attention?
  1. Many of the guidelines Taylor and others devised appear to be common sense.
  2. To understand the importance of scientific management, you have to consider the times.
     a)
     b)
     c)
     d)

E. What Did Henri Fayol and Max Weber Contribute to Management Thought?
  1. Fayol wrote during the same time as Taylor.
     a) Taylor was concerned with
     b) Fayol's attention was directed at
     c) Fayol was
  2. Fayol described management as
     a) He argued that
     b) He stated fourteen principles of management — fundamental or universal truths.
        (1) These principles are shown in Exhibit HM-2.
  3. Max Weber was a German sociologist.
     a) Writing in
     b) He described an ideal type of organization, the bureaucracy.

F. What Were the General Administrative Theorists' Contributions to Management Practice?
  1. A number of our current ideas and practices in management can be directly traced to the contributions of the general administrative theorists.
     a) The functional view of the manager's job owes its origin to
  2. Weber's bureaucracy was an attempt to
     a) It was a response to
     b) Weber believed that his model could

IV. HUMAN RESOURCES APPROACH
A. Who Were Some Early Advocates of the Human Resources Approach?
  1. Five individuals stand out as early advocates of the human resources approach

B. What Claim to Fame Does Robert Owen Hold?
  1. A successful
  2. Repulsed by
  3. He argued that
  4. Owen proposed a

C. For What Is Hugo Munsterberg Best Known?
  1. The creator of the field of
  2. His text, *Psychology and Industrial Efficiency*, published in 1913.
     a) He argued for
     b) Suggested the use of
     c) He saw a link between
     d) Much of our current knowledge of

D. What Contributions Did Mary Parker Follett Make to Management?
  1. One of the earliest writers to view organizations in terms of individual and group behavior.
  2. A transitionalist, Follett was a

3. Organizations should be based on
    a) Individual potential
4. The manager's job was to
5. Managers and workers should view themselves as
    a) Managers should
    b) Her humanistic ideas influenced

E. Who Was Chester Barnard?

1. A transitionalist like Follett.
    a) His ideas bridged
2. Like Fayol, Barnard was
    a) The president of
3. He had read Weber.
    a) Barnard saw organizations as
    b) He expressed his views in his book
4. Organizations were made up of people who
    a) The manager's major roles were to
    b) An organization's success depended largely on
    c) Also, success depended on maintaining
5. The current interest in building

F. What Were the Hawthorne Studies?

1. The most important contribution to the human resources approach.
    a) Studies undertaken at
2. Originally begun in
3. Devised by
    a) Control and experimental groups were established.
    b) The experimental group was
    c) The engineers expected
    d) To the surprise of the engineers
    e) In fact,
    f) The engineers concluded that
4. In 1927, the Western Electric engineers asked
    a) This relationship lasted through
    b) The results
    c) Social norms, or standards of the group, were
5. The Hawthorne studies
    a) Mayo's conclusions
    b) They also led to
6. The Hawthorne studies have been criticized.
    a)
    b)
7. The legacy of Hawthorne is still with us today.
    a) Current organizational practices

G. Why Was the Human Relations Movement Important to Management History?

1. Members of this movement
    a) Dale Carnegie, Abraham Maslow, and Douglas McGregor.
    b) Their views were shaped
2. Dale Carnegie is
    a) *How to Win Friends and Influence People,*

        b) During this same period
        c) The theme of Carnegie's book and lectures
   3. Abraham Maslow
        a) Maslow argued that
        b) An early 1970s survey of management professors found that
        c) The needs hierarchy is
   4. Douglas McGregor,
        a) Theory X presents
        b) Theory Y offers
        c) He believed that Theory Y
        d) McGregor had taught (at MIT) and then became
        e) The irony,
        f) McGregor's beliefs about human nature

H. What Was the Common Thread That Linked Advocates of the Human Relations Movement?
   1. An unshakable optimism about
   2. They believed strongly

I. Who Were the Behavioral Science Theorists?
   1. A group of
        a) These theorists engaged in
        b) They sought to
   2. A list of important behavioral science theorists would
        a) Beginning after World War II, they
        b) Our current understanding of such issues as

V. THE QUANTITATIVE APPROACH
A. Its Origins
   1. This approach to management (operations research or management science) evolved out of
        a) The British
        b) U.S. antisubmarine warfare teams
   2. After the war, many of the quantitative techniques
   3. One group of military officers, labeled the "Whiz Kids,"
        a) Two of the most famous
        b) McNamara rose to
        c) Tex Thornton founded
        d) The consulting firm of Arthur D. Little

B. What Are the Quantitative Techniques, and How Have They Contributed to Current Management Practice?
   1. This approach includes applications of
        a) Linear programming
        b) Work scheduling
   2. In general, the quantitative approaches have

VI. ANALYSIS: HOW TIMES SHAPE MANAGEMENT APPROACHES
A. What Stimulated the Classical Approach?
   1. The common thread was
   2. The world of the late nineteenth and early twentieth century was one of
        a) Most organizational activities

     b) Job responsibilities were
     c) Managers, when they existed, had
  3. The standardized practices offered by the classicists
  4. Production was
     a) So Taylor could justify
     b) Similarly, Gilbreth's breakthroughs
  5. The application of scientific management principles contributed to

B. What Stimulated the Human Resources Approach?
  1. The human resources approach really began
  2. Two related forces.
     a) First
     b) Second
  3. The classical view
  4. This kind of thinking created
  5. The human resources approach offered
  6. The Great Depression
     a) The New Deal
     b) The Social Security Act was
     c) The National Labor Relations Act
     d) The Fair Labor Standards Act
     e) The Railroad Unemployment Insurance Act
  7. Humanizing the workplace had become congruent with society's concerns at the time.

C. What Stimulated the Quantitative Approaches?
  1. The major impetus to the quantitative approaches was
  2. After the war,
     a) As these techniques worked
  3. New organizations were created to
     a) The Operations Research Society of America was founded
     b) In 1953, The Institute of Management Science.
  4. By the late-1960s

VII. BUILDING ON HISTORY: STUDYING MANAGEMENT TODAY
A. What Is the Process Approach?
  1. In December 1961, Professor Harold Koontz
     a) While each of the diverse approaches
  2. He felt that a process approach could
  3. The process approach, originally introduced by
     a) Refer back to Exhibit 1-4.
  4. Although Koontz's article stimulated considerable debate,

B. How Can a Systems Approach Integrate Management Concepts?
  1. The systems approach defines a system as
     a) Societies are
  2. There are two basic types of systems
     a)
     b)
     c) See Exhibit HM-4.
  3. An organization (and its management) is
     a) We call this relationship

b) Stakeholders represent
c) The manager's job is to
4. The systems approach recognizes that
   a) Organizational survival often depends on
   b) These include
5. The systems approach appears to be
6. Although the systems perspective does not provide

C. What Is a Contingency Approach to the Study of Management?
1. The contingency approach
2. A contingency approach to the study of management is
3. Advocates of the contingency approach
4. Exhibit HM-5 describes four popular contingency variables.
5. This list is not comprehensive — there are at least 100 different variables identified — but it represents those most widely used.

REVIEW QUESTIONS
1. What was Fredrick Taylor's contribution to management theory? What other theorists did he influence?
   Answer – Pages 29-30

2. Who were the major contributors to human resources approach, and what were their individual contributions to this school of thought?
   Answer – Pages 33-36

3. How does a quantitative approach differ from human resources/human relations approach?
   Answer – Pages 38-39

4. How did society and time in history affect the development of each major school of management thought?
   Answer – Pages 39-40

5. In what ways does a systems approach integrate other management theories?
   Answer – Pages 41-42

STUDY QUIZ
Multiple Choice Questions
1. The concept of the division of labor originally came from the work of:
   a) Fredrick Taylor.
   b) Max Weber.
   c) Adam Smith.
   d) Chester Barnard.

2. The classical management theorist most concerned with efficiency and who sought it by selecting and matching workers to their jobs and then training them was:
   a) Frank Gilbreath.
   b) Fredrick Taylor.
   c) Henry Gantt.
   d) Henri Fayol.

3. The importance of scientific management to management practice lay in its:
   a) humanity and focus on the development of the individual worker.
   b) impartiality and impersonal nature of the management process.
   c) organizing hierarchy providing a clear chain of command.
   d) improving the standard of living and working conditions.

4. The early management theorist who was bothered by the severe treatment of workers, argued the owners should treat their workers at least as well as their equipment, and who argued that investing in workers was both highly profitable and the right thing to do was:
   a) the human resources theorist, Robert Owen.
   b) the general administrative theorist, Max Weber.
   c) the classical theorist, Henry Gantt.
   d) the contemporary theorist, Chester Barnard.

5. Seeking to bridge classical and human resources approaches to management, _____ , influenced by Max Weber, argued that organizations were made up of people who have interacting social relationships.
   a) Robert Owen
   b) Chester Barnard
   c) Elton Mayo
   d) Dale Carnegie

6. _____ is the most widely known management theory and was proposed by _____ even though there is no empirical evidence supporting this theory.
   a) Theory X and Theory Y, Douglas McGregor
   b) Quantitative theory, Robert Thornton
   c) Hierarchy of needs, Abraham Maslow
   d) Hawthorne Studies, Elton Mayo

7. The management theory that was rather subjective in its unshakeable optimism in human nature and individual capability, even to the point of not accepting contrary research, was the:
   a) quantitative approach.
   b) human relations movement.
   c) human resources approach.
   d) general administrative approach.

8. The quantitative approach to management grew out of:
   a) extensive social science research by academic management theorists.
   b) the practical experiences of the executives of large corporations.
   c) the earlier work of Fredrick Taylor and Henry Gantt and classical management theory.
   d) the use of statistical solutions to operational problems during World War II.

9. The emergence of the Great Depression and a strong reaction to the mechanistic way people were being managed encouraged the development of the:
   a) classical approach to management theory.
   b) general administrative approach to management theory.
   c) human resources approach to management theory.
   d) contemporary approach to management theory.

10. When Professor Harold Koontz wrote an article summarizing the various approaches to management, he also offered a _____ approach as a way to synthesize and encompass all of the diversity of these various approaches.
    a) process
    b) quantitative
    c) systems
    d) contingency

True/False Questions

1. Management theory first took form during the late 18th century during the industrial revolution as Rockefeller and Carnegie created their business empires in the United States

2. Henri Fayol and Max Weber turned management into a general set of principles and tried to create the ideal model organization in their writings.

3. The field of Industrial Psychology owes its beginnings to the work of Hugo Munsterberg and his scientific study of individuals in order to improve productivity.

4. The Hawthorne studies have a significant impact on management thought in redirecting managers from a focus on money as incentive to a greater consideration of the human factors involved in organizational success.

5. Often ignored as a management theorist, Douglas McGregor wrote *How to Win Friends and Influence People* and influenced new and experienced managers alike from the 1930s to the 1950s.

6. A management approach, based on the use of scientific method to study organizational behavior and human motivation impartially and empirically, was the behavioral science theorists.

7. Classical management theory brought order to chaos, efficiency to inefficiency, and standardized practices improving productivity to a largely unstructured management world.

8. The quantitative approach to management was stimulated by the negative reaction of employers and employees to the more mechanistic style of classical management theory.

9. Jonathan is thinking about the stakeholders in his organization, his company's interaction with its external environment, and how the various units in his company work together to generate their products. Jonathan's perspective represents a process approach to management.

10. Contingency management theory is intuitively logical, integrates a number of management approaches, and adapts a manager's solutions and actions to the various factors involved in a given situation.

Answers to Chapter 1a Study Quiz

Multiple Choice (Page - Answer)

1. c-28   6. c-37
2. b-29   7. b-36
3. d-30   8. d-38
4. a-34   9. c-39
5. b-35   10. a-41

True/False

1. F-27   6. T-38
2. T-32   7. T-39
3. T-34   8. F-40
4. T-35   9. F-41
5. F-36   10. T-42

CHAPTER 2 - MANAGING IN TODAY'S WORLD

LEARNING OUTCOMES

After reading this chapter, you should be able to:

1. Describe the three waves in modern social history and their implications for organizations.
2. Explain the importance of viewing management from a global perspective. Identify how technology is changing the manager's job.
3. Define social responsibility and ethics.
4. Explain what is meant by the term *entrepreneurial spirit*.
5. Describe the management implications of a diversified workforce.
6. Explain why companies focus on quality and continuous improvement.
7. Describe why many corporations have downsized.

Use the Outline to Guide Your Note Taking from the Text

Considerations as you read

As you read and take notes, think about these questions; they will help you organize your study notes.

1. How has the business environment changed over the last 40 years?
2. How do international organizations and international management differ from their domestic counterparts?
3. In what ways does technology shape the manager's task?
4. What part does social responsibility play in the management of organizations?
5. Why is everyone so excited about the entrepreneurial spirit?
6. What will the future workforce look like, and what are the implications for management?
7. How do organizations make the customer king?

I. **THE CHANGING ECONOMY**
    A. **Introduction**
        1. The 1960s show
            a) See Exhibit 2-1
        2. One of the biggest problems in managing an organization is
            a) Just 25 years ago,
            b) E-mail and modems,
            c) Computers often took up expansive space, quite unlike the 4-pound laptop today.
            d) The silicon chip and other advances
        3. Alvin Toffler
        4. He argued that
            a) The first wave was driven by agriculture.
            b) The second wave was industrialization.
        5. By the start of the 1970's a new age was gaining momentum, based on
            a) Technological advancements were
            b) The information wave was transforming
            c) Job growth in the past 20 years has been
            d) Knowledge workers are
            e) The number of blue-collar workers
            f) Some of the blue-collar workers don't
        6. These waves also affect how we do business.
            a) See Exhibit 2-2.

II. A GLOBAL MARKET PLACE
A. The Globalization of Business
1. Management is no longer constrained by
   a) BMW,
   b) McDonald's
   c) The world has become
2. To be effective in this boundaryless world
3. In the 1960s, Canada's prime minister
   a) In the 2000s,
4. International businesses
   a)
   b)
   c)
5. The generic global organization, the transnational corporation (TNC).
   a) Decisions in TNCs
   b) Nationals are
   c) The products and marketing strategies
   d) Nestles,
6. The borderless organization
   a) IBM
   b) Ford

B. How Does Globalization Affect Organizations?
1. An organization going global typically
2. In stage I,
   a) This is
   b) The organization
3. In Stage II,
   a) Still
   b) Sales through
   c) To manufacture,
4. Stage III,
   a) As shown in Exhibit 2-3,
   b) License or franchise
   c) Joint ventures
   d) The greatest commitment (and risk),

C. What Effect Does Globalization Have on Managers?
1. Whirlpool
2. In the changing global environment,
   a)
   b)
   c)
3. A boundaryless world introduces
4. One specific challenge,
5. U.S. managers in the past held
6. Countries have different
7. Traditional approaches to international business sought
   a) Organizational success
   b) Example
   c) Countries also have differences in their laws.

8. Viewing the global environment
9. A more appropriate approach is
10. A study of the differences of cultural environments was conducted by
    a) He surveyed
    b) Hofstede's data indicated that
    c) He classified those values and attitudes into four specific dimensions of national culture.
    d) See Exhibit 2-4.
11. Implications
    a)
    b)
12. Most cross-cultural encounters are
    a) A manager must understand that
        (1) The Mars company (the candy maker) example.
    b) Managers need to be

III. EMPHASIS ON TECHNOLOGY
A. Introduction
1. Suppose you need information on how well your unit is meeting its production standards.
    a) Thirty years ago
    b) Today,
2. Since the 1970s, U.S. companies
    a) These technologies
3. Technology includes
    a) Technological advances reflect
    b) Technology made it possible to
    c) Technology is making it possible to
4. Technological advancements are also
    a) Most cars
    b) And at Frito-Lay,

B. How Does an Organization Benefit from Information Technology?
1. Technological changes, especially IT changes,
2. IT has created the ability to
3. One important implication is that
4. Another implication is that
5. E-commerce,
    a) Organizations are using the Internet to
6. E-commerce is
    a) In 1998,
    b) 16 percent of all car buyers in
    c) The fastest growing stocks on Wall Street
    d) One of the greatest effects is

C. In What Ways Does Technology Alter a Manager's Job?
1. Technology changed the manager's job.
2. Organizations today have become
3. Managers can get
    a) Information technology enhanced
4. Technology is also
    a) Historically,
    b) Management could

c) Managers are able to
d) Many employers no longer
5. Management's two biggest challenges
a) Addressing these challenges will focus on
b) The emphasis will be on

IV. WHAT DOES SOCIETY EXPECT FROM ORGANIZATIONS AND THEIR MANAGERS?

A. Introduction
1. The importance of corporate social responsibility surfaced in
2. Before
a) See Exhibit 2-5.
3. Managers are now confronted with
4. In a globally competitive world,
5. Few terms have been defined in as many different ways as social responsibility.
6. Some of the more popular meanings.
a)
b)
c)
d)
e)
7. The debate has focused at the extremes.
a) The classical
b) The socioeconomic position

B. How Can Organizations Demonstrate Socially Responsible Actions?
1. Social responsibility is
a) This definition assumes that
b) This definition views business as
2. Comparison with two similar concepts
a)
b)
3. Social responsibility
4. Social responsiveness
5. Social responsibility requires
6. Social responsiveness is guided by

C. How Do Managers Become More Socially Responsible?
1. Ethics commonly refers to
a) Exhibit 2-6 presents three views of ethical standards.
2. Whether a manager acts ethically or unethically will depend on several factors, including:
a)
b)
c)
d)
e)
3. People who lack
4. Codes of ethics are
a) A formal document that
b) Nearly 90 percent of
5. The effectiveness of ethical codes depends

V. WHY THE EMPHASIS ON THE ENTREPRENEURIAL SPIRIT?

A. Introduction
1. As the environment surrounding business continues to
2. It's also happening in

B. Its Origins
1. Entrepreneurship is the process of
   a) Because they usually start
2. Why the increased popularity?
   a) There has always been
   b) Recent changes in

C. Intrapreneurship
1. The entrepreneurial spirit is not limited solely to the small business.
2. Some companies are attempting to model the activities of the entrepreneur.
   a) Entrepreneurs are
   b) The owner-manager is
   c) The owner-manager is
3. Intrapreneurs — people who
   a) Can entrepreneurs exist in
   b) The answer depends on
4. Peter Drucker argues that
   a) An entrepreneurial manager is
   b) Contrasted with the traditional manager
   c) Drucker's use of the term entrepreneurial is
5. We will come back to entrepreneurs in the next chapter.

VI. WHAT WILL THE WORKFORCE OF 2010 LOOK LIKE?
A. The Melting Pot
1. Until very recently,
2. They assumed that
3. Managers found that
4. The melting-pot assumption is

B. How Does Diversity Affect Organizations?
1. More diverse diversity leads to
2. Many organizations today
   a)
   b)
3. Some, like Motorola, actually
4. Other organizations are
5. Some organizations, such as
   a) These include a wide range of
6. With more women working and more two-career couples,
   a) Studies indicate that

C. How Do We Make Managers More Sensitive to Differences?
1. The diversity that exists in the workforce requires
2. Managers need to recognize
3. Of course, they must not

4. Such organizations as
    a) These programs are designed to

VII. HOW DO ORGANIZATIONS MAKE THE CUSTOMER KING?
A. Introduction
1. Henry Ford said his customers
2. Stew Leonard,
    a) Rule 1-
    b) Rule 2-
3. Managers are being influenced by
    a) Long-term success
    b) Customers have
    c) Customers are
4. Mass customization,

B. How Have Organizations Shown an Increased Concern with Quality?
1. There is a quality revolution.
    a) The generic term that has evolved to
    b) Inspired by quality experts like
2. An American,
    a) In 1950,
    b) Central to his methods,
    c) A well-managed organization was one
3. Deming developed a fourteen-point program for transforming organizations.
4. Today, Deming's original program
    a) See Exhibit 2-7.
5. TQM expands the term *customer* to
    a) The objective is to create
6. Criticized by some for
    a) Example of Varian Associates, Inc., a maker of scientific equipment.
    b) Example of Globe Metallurgical Inc., a small Ohio metal producer.
    c) Example, the significant improvements in the quality of cars produced by GM, Ford, and DaimlerChrysler can be directly traced to the implementation of total quality methods.

C. Why Must Managers Think in Terms of Quantum Changes Rather Than Continuous Improvement?
1. Continuous improvement methods
2. Such action
3. Many organizations, however,
    a) A focus on continuous improvements may
    b) Incremental change may
    c) Continuous change may also
4. Aren't these contradictory statements?
    a) Continuous improvement can
    b) That's the case if
    c) Then continuous improvement can have its rightful place.
5. Roller skate business example, continuous improvement approach.
    a) Frame of reference,
    b) Your focus
6. A competitor reengineers the design process.
    a) Your competitor asks,

        b) Starting from scratch,
        c) You are now competing against
    7. In this contrived example, both companies made progress.
        a) But
    8. Our example demonstrates

D. Why Do Organizations Lay Off Workers?
    1. Corporate America used to follow a simple rule
    2. Since the late 1980s
        a) IBM
        b) Boeing
    3. Jobs are
        a) For example,
    4. Organizations are attempting to
    5. Continuous improvement and work process
        a) The result is
    6. Downsizing
    7. A better term might be
        a) AT&T

E. How Do Organizations Create Flexible and Rapid Response Systems?
    1. Lou Capolzzola example.
    2. Thousands of organizations are
        a) See Exhibit 2-8.
    3. Many large companies are
    4. Organizations facing a rapidly changing environment must
        a)
        b)
    5. Opportunities to capitalize on new markets,
        a) Nearly 2 decades
        b) Today that number is
    6. In Europe,
        a) About
    7. Many employees have indicated
        a) Yet the prime reason United Parcel Service's 185,000 workers went on strike

F. What Issues Do Contingent Workers Create for Managers?
    1. Each contingent worker
    2. Managers must also make sure that
    3. They may not be
    4. Today's managers need to

VIII. SOME CONCLUDING REMARKS
    1. Both organizations and managers need to
    2. Frederick Taylor, the "father of scientific management" argued
    3. Workers today are
        a) Today's workers may be
    4. Managers are
        a) Managers are finding that
        b) Managers also recognize that
    5. We call this process

6. The movement is being driven by two forces.
   a) First
   b) Second
7. Letting go and stretching can be likened to the role of a sports team coach.
   a)
   b)
   c)
   d)
   e)
8. This coaching role is

REVIEW QUESTIONS

1. Describe the shifts in the types of jobs in the workforce during the past 100 years.
   Answer – Pages 47-48

2. Explain the managerial implications of a global village.
   Answer – Pages 49-50

3. Discuss the various forms a corporation can take when it competes in the global market.
   Answer – Pages 49-51

4. How does technology shape organizations and affect the job of the manager?
   Answer – Pages 54-57

5. What part does social responsibility play in the task of management in an organization? What expectations does society have of its managers today?
   Answer – Pages 57-60

6. Why are organizations emphasizing entrepreneurship and intrapreneurship? How do these concepts differ?
   Answer – Page 61

7. Describe the managerial implications of growing organizational diversity.
   Answer – Page 63

8. How does the quality movement affect management practice in organizations? Is the impact different for each technique? If so, why?
   Answer – Page 64

9. How are rightsizing, the use of contingency workers, and the empowerment movement reshaping the manager's job in the 21st century?
   Answer – Pages 68-69

STUDY QUIZ
Multiple Choice Questions

1. The third wave of the evolution of civilization is noted for:
   a) the acquisition and application of information.
   b) people who were their own bosses, performing a variety of tasks.
   c) routine work within standardized processes heavily dependent on human power.
   d) the use of permanent highly trained workers paid on the basis of productivity.

2. Techtronics operates units in a number of different countries, making decisions on the local level, using nations to run operations within those countries, and tailoring products and marketing strategies to the individual country's culture. It is an example of a/an:
   a) multinational corporation.
   b) strategic alliances.
   c) transnational corporation.
   d) borderless corporation.

3. In Stage III of the globalization of a company, a firm might form joint ventures with foreign companies to share the cost of developing new products or building production facilities in a foreign country. These newly formed companies are known as:
   a) multinational corporations.
   b) strategic alliances.
   c) transnational corporations.
   d) borderless corporations.

4. Hofstede's study of employees working in foreign countries identified four cultural dimensions. That dimension that deals with the social framework in which people look after their own interests and those of their immediate family is:
   a) individualism.
   b) power distance.
   c) uncertainty theory.
   d) quantity vs. quality of life.

5. _____ is the use of tools, equipment, and/or operating methods to make work more efficient.
   a) Parochialism
   b) Information technology
   c) Telecommuting
   d) Technology

6. The use of the Internet to transmit and process data in order to facilitate business is known as:
   a) information technology.
   b) telecommuting.
   c) e-commerce.
   d) technology.

7. Technology will impact the manager's job in a number of ways, including:
   a) increasing the need to train managers on performance standards and ensuring quality.
   b) radically changing compensation and incentive strategies used to motivate employees.
   c) dramatically decreasing the need to be socially conscious.
   d) all of these.

8. Cudro is thinking through the rules and principles that define right and wrong conduct within his company. Cudro is thinking about:
   a) his company's social obligation to society.
   b) the concept of social responsibility.
   c) a code of ethics.
   d) ethics.

9. Which of the following is true about entrepreneurship in today's management world?
   a) Few entrepreneurial businesses are actually small businesses.
   b) Franchising is significantly boosting the growth in entrepreneurship.
   c) It is largely an American and European phenomenon.
   d) Entrepreneurship is simply the same thing as good management practice.

10. The management concept or theory that expands the definition of a customer to everyone involved with the organization, internally or externally, employees, suppliers, etc., is know as:
   a) re-engineering.
   b) social responsibility.
   c) total quality management.
   d) work process engineering.

11. Total quality management is an excellent change process but it has several inherent dangers such as:
   a) not leading the organization to the right type of organizational change.
   b) focusing on incremental product change rather than radical system change.
   c) not making sufficient change to keep current with competitors' improvements.
   d) all of these.

12. When a company manages the size of its workforce by closely linking staffing levels to organizational goals, the firm is involved in:
   a) rightsizing.
   b) downsizing.
   c) work process engineering.
   d) contingency workforce management.

13. A number of factors are pushing companies toward the greater use of contingency workers including:
   a) giving managers more options for dealing with changes in market cycles.
   b) providing organizations with greater flexibility.
   c) decreasing the complexity of layoff decisions and forecasting their impact on productivity.
   d) all of these.

14. The use of contingency workers can actually be a good thing for workers because:
   a) it completely eliminates the threat of job loss due to strikes or layoffs.
   b) many people choose to be contingency workers because of the variety involved in the job.
   c) they generally get paid much better and have better benefit packages than full-time workers.
   d) contingency jobs almost always translate into full-time positions.

15. When managers redesign jobs to increase decision-making discretion for workers, they are:
   a) moving to a contingency workforce.
   b) using a classical management style.
   c) empowering employees.
   d) rightsizing.

True/False Questions
1. According to Alvin Toffle, the second wave of the evolution of civilization was industrialization.

2. In international business, the type of organization which maintains significant operations in two or more countries but is still based in one home country is a transnational corporation (TNC).

3. If Alicia commits her firm to make and/or sell products in other countries by using domestic sales professionals sent to the foreign countries or using foreign sales reps, her company is in Stage III of the globalization process.

4. In terms of Hofstede's cultural dimensions, those countries most like the United States in terms of power distance and individualism are Colombia, Philippines, and Singapore.

5. The spread of information technology is lessening the need for skilled and educated workers because computers do more and more of the thinking for workers.

6. Social responsibility is the obligation of a firm, beyond legality, to pursue long-term goals that are good for society.

7. The ethicality of a manager's behavior depends on a number of factors that may change with any given situation.

8. Nearly 2 million people are starting their own businesses annually within the United States.

9. When companies offer "family-friendly" benefits, it is because it is the right thing to do, because such benefit plans have little practical impact on productivity, absenteeism, or employee retention.

10. Reengineering is like TQM in its focus on gradual incremental change within an organization.

11. TQM has an impressive record for improving productivity and quality in organizations.

12. Work process engineering is a process that permits organizations to make more radical changes and progress in a dynamic business, than a TQM process.

13. When a company reduces its workforce in order to make it more closely fit its organizational goals, it is empowering its workforce.

14. The contingency workforce is largely only an issue in technology and information management.

15. Today, there are nearly 619,000 temporary jobs in the United States and Europe, a small decrease from 20 years ago.

Answers to Chapter 2 Study Quiz

Multiple Choice (Page - Answer)

1. a-48	6. c-55	11. d-65
2. c-50	7. a-56	12. a-67
3. b-51	8. d-59	13. d-68
4. a-53	9. b-61	14. b-69
5. d-54	10. c-64	15. c-70

True/False

1.T-48	6. T-57	11. T-64
2. F-50	7. T-60	12. T-65
3. F-51	8. T-61	13. F-67
4. F-53	9. F-63	14. F-68
5. F-55	10. F-64	15. F-68

PART 2: PLANNING
CHAPTER 3 - FOUNDATIONS OF PLANNING

LEARNING OUTCOMES
After studying this chapter, you should be able to:
1. Define planning.
2. Explain the potential benefits of planning.
3. Identify potential drawbacks to planning.
4. Distinguish between strategic and tactical plans.
5. State when directional plans are preferred over specific plans.
6. Define management by objectives, and identify its common elements.
7. Outline the steps in the strategic management process.
8. Describe the four grand strategies.
9. Explain SWOT analysis.
10. Compare how entrepreneurs and bureaucratic managers approach strategy.

Use the Outline to Guide Your Note Taking from the Text

Considerations as you read
As you read and take note, think about these questions; they will help you organize your study notes.

1. What are the benefits and drawbacks of formal planning?
2. How are plans used in organizations?
3. Describe the MBO process and its use in the management of people.
4. Outline the strategic planning process.
5. How can management use quality as a strategic weapon?
6. How does entrepreneurship influence and shape the strategic planning process?

I. **PLANNING DEFINED**
   A. **Introduction**
      1. It encompasses
         a) It is concerned with
      2. Planning can be further defined in terms of
         a) In informal planning
      3. Planning establishes
         a)
      4. Planning reduces
      5. It clarifies
      6. It is precisely
      7. Planning also
      8. Finally, planning establishes

   B. **What Are Some Criticisms of Formal Planning?**
      1. Formal planning became very popular in the 1960s, and still is today.
         a) Critics
      2. Planning may
         a) Formal planning efforts
         b) The assumption
         c) Example
      3. Plans can't be
         a) Today's business environment

        b)   That means
        c)   Managing chaos and turning disasters into opportunities requires
    4. Formal plans can't replace
        a)   Visions have a tendency to
        b)   Formal planning efforts typically
    5. Planning focuses managers' attention on
        a)   The focus
        b)   It often does not
    6. Formal planning reinforces
        a)   Success may
        b)   It is hard to
        c)   Successful plans may

C. The Bottom Line: Does Planning Improve Organizational Performance?
    1. The evidence
    2. However, organizations that formally plan
    3. Conclusions
        a)
        b)
        c)

II. TYPES OF PLANS
A. Exhibit 3-2

B. How Do Strategic and Tactical Planning Differ?
    1. Strategic plans apply to
        a)   These plans drive
        b)   They serve as
    2. Tactical plans
    3. Strategic and tactical plans differ in three primary ways.
        a)
        b)
        c)

C. In What Time Frame Do Plans Exist?
    1. Short-term covers
    2. Any time frame beyond five years is
    3. The difference between short- and long-term plans is
        a)
        b)
        c)

D. What Is the Difference between Specific and Directional Plans?
    1. It appears intuitively correct that
        a)   Specific plans have
    2. Specific plans are not
        a)   They require
    3. When uncertainty is high
        a)   See Exhibit 3-3.
    4. Directional plans
        a)   They provide

E. How Do Single-Use and Standing Plans Differ?
    1. A single-use plan is
        a) Example
    2. Standing plans are
        a) Example

III. MANAGEMENT BY OBJECTIVES
A. What Is MBO?
    1. Management by objectives is
    2. Its appeal is its emphasis
    3. MBO makes objectives
        a) See Exhibit 3-4.
        b) MBO works from
        c) The result is
        d) For the individual employee

B. What Are the Common Elements to an MBO Program?
    1. There are four ingredients common to MBO programs.
    2.
    3.
    4.

C. Does MBO Work?
    1. Assessing the effectiveness of MBO is a complex task.
    2. When a person's ability and acceptance of goals are held constant
        a) Specific hard goals
        b) Feedback
        c) These results are
        d) MBO is most effective if
    3. There is little relationship between
        a) When goal difficulty is held constant
        b) It is not possible to
        c) One major benefit of participation
    4. Studies of actual MBO programs confirm that
        a) Top management commitment

D. How Do You Set Employee Objectives?
    1. Every manager can
        a)
        b)
        c)
        d)
        e)
        f)

E. Is There a Downside to Objectives?
    1. Not everyone
    2. One of the most vocal critics was
        a) Deming felt that
        b) Deming believed that
    3. Specific goals also

4. Specific goals may
5. How can the criticisms of objectives be overcome?
    a)
    b)
    c)

IV. THE IMPORTANCE OF AN ORGANIZATIONAL STRATEGY
A. Before the Early 1970s
1. Managers generally assumed that better times lay ahead.
2. Plans for the future were merely extensions of where the organization had been in the past.

B. The 1970s and 1980s
1. However,
2. These changes forced
3.
4.

C. Today
1. One survey of business owners found that
2. Other studies support the premise that
3. Strategic planning has moved beyond

V. A STRATEGIC FRAMEWORK: CHOOSING A NICHE
A. The Strategic Management Process
1. See Exhibit 3-5.
2. A nine-step process that involves strategic planning, implementation, and evaluation.
3. Strategic planning encompasses the first seven steps.

B. How Does the Strategic Management Process Operate?
1. First, identify the
    a)
    b)
2. Analyze the environment (step 2).
    a)
    b)
    c) Step 2 is complete when
3. What is environmental scanning?
    a) The screening
    b) There is some evidence
    c) The importance of environmental scanning was
4. How is competitive intelligence useful?
    a) It seeks
    b) 95 percent of the competitor-related information
5. In a global business environment, these processes are more complex.
    a)
    b)

C. What Are the Primary Steps in the Strategic Management Process?
1. Evaluate (step 3)
    a) Opportunities are
    b) Threats are

        c)   The same environment can present
  2. Next, in step 4, we evaluate the organization's internal resources.
        a)   Every organization is
        b)   The analysis should lead
        c)   It should also indicate
  3. Step 5, strengths are internal resources available or things that the organization does well.
        a)   Core competencies are
        b)   Weaknesses are
        c)   Strong and weak cultures have
            (1) In a strong culture
            (2) In a strong culture
            (3) The negative side of a strong culture
            (4) A strong culture may act as

D. What Is SWOT Analysis?
  1. A merging of the externalities (steps 2 and 3) with the internalities (steps 4 and 5).
        a)   See Exhibit 3-6.
  2. Called SWOT analysis because
  3. Having completed the SWOT analysis
        a)   Exhibit 3-5, step 6.
        b)   Example, Kodak international sales.

E. How Do You Formulate Strategies?
  1. Strategies need to be set for all levels in the organization (step 7).
  2. Four primary strategies or grand strategies are available
  3. The growth strategy
        a)
        b)
        c)
  4. The stability strategy
        a)
        b)
        c)
        d)
  5. The retrenchment strategy
        a)
        b)
        c)
  6. The combination strategy
        a)
        b)
        c)
  7. Determining a competitive strategy
        a)   The selection of a grand strategy sets the stage for the entire organization.
        b)   Each unit within
        c)   To fulfill the grand strategy
        d)   This positioning requires
  8. Michael Porter of Harvard's Graduate School of Business.
        a)   His competitive strategies framework
        b)   No firm can successfully perform at
        c)   Management must select

       d)   These three strategies are:
9. The low-cost producer in its industry,
    a)
    b)
    c)
10. A differentiation strategy,
    a)
    b)
    c)
11. The first two strategies sought a competitive advantage in
12. The focus strategy aims at
    a)
    b)
    c)
    d)
13. Strategy choice depends on
    a)   The organization should
14. If an organization cannot use one of these
    a)   Porter uses the term
    b)   Organizations that are
15. Sustaining a competitive advantage
    a)   Long-term success requires
    b)   It must withstand both
    c)   Managers need to create
    d)   When there are

F. What Happens after Strategies Are Formulated?
    1. The next-to-last step in the strategic management process is
        a)   A strategic plan
        b)   Top management leadership is
    2. Finally, results must be
        a)
        b)

VI. QUALITY AS A STRATEGIC WEAPON
A. Quality Practices as a Competitive Advantage
    1. To the degree that an organization can
    2. Constant improvement in
        a)   Product innovations are not
    3. Incremental improvement is
        a)   Example,

B. How Can Benchmarking Help Promote Quality?
    1. Benchmarking involves
    2. Management can
        a)   It is a very specific form of
    3. In 1979, Xerox
        a)   Until then, the Japanese
        b)   Xerox's head of manufacturing
    4. Illustrating benchmarking's use in practice, Ford Motor Company.
        a)   Ford used benchmarking

C. What Is the ISO 9000 Series?
1. The 1980s,
2. In 1987, the formation of
   a) The ISO standards reflect
3. These standards assure customers that:
   a)
   b)
   c)
   d)
4. Examples of the multinational and transnational companies that have met these standards.
   a)
   b)
   c)
5. A company that obtains an ISO certification can
6. Certification also permits
   a)
   b)
7. Most organizations that want certification
   a) Example, Betz Laboratories in Trevor, Pennsylvania,

D. How Can Attaining Six Sigma Signify Quality?
1. Six sigma is a
   a) The premise,
   b) Six sigma attempts to
   c) It is a process that
2. Effectiveness of six sigma at ensuring quality.
   a) It is designed to
   b) Three sigma
3. How have organizations that have implemented six sigma methodologies fared?
   a) Example of AlliedSignal
   b) GE

VII. ENTREPRENEURSHIP: A SPECIAL CASE OF STRATEGIC PLANNING
A. Story
1. Linda Lang founded
2. She started her company after
3. Lang has built
4. Strategic planning often
   a) It implies

B. What Is Entrepreneurship?
1. Various definitions.
   a) The creation of any new business.
   b) Entrepreneurs seek to
   c) When most people describe entrepreneurs, they
2. The text defines entrepreneurship as
3. Managing a small business is
   a)
   b)
   c)

C. Do Entrepreneurs Possess Similar Characteristics?
  1. A number of common characteristics have been found.
      a)
      b)
      c)
      d)
      e)
  2. Three factors regularly sit on the top of most lists.
      a) Entrepreneurs have a high need for
      b) They believe strongly that
      c) They take
  3. The research allows us to draw a general description of entrepreneurs.
      a) They tend to be
      b) They plan
      c) Entrepreneurs also value
      d) Entrepreneurs prefer to take
  4. The evidence on entrepreneurial personalities leads us to several conclusions.
      a) First, people with this personality makeup
      b) Second, the challenges and conditions inherent in
      c) Finally, the cultural context

D. How Do Entrepreneurs Compare with Traditional Managers?
  1. Exhibit 3-8 summarizes some key differences.
  2. The latter tend to be

REVIEW QUESTIONS

1. How does formal planning help and hinder managers in performing their jobs?
   Answer – Pages 81-82

2. Create a chart of the different types of plans, their uses, and who uses each type of plan.
   Answer – Pages 84-86

3. What is MBO, and how does it assist the manager in directing the work of his/her subordinates?
   Answer – Pages 86-88

4. What is the role of environmental scanning and developing competitive intelligence in the strategic process?
   Answer – Pages 91-92

5. Outline and explain the various elements of the strategic management process.
   Answer – Pages 93-98

6. What is a SWOT analysis? How is it used in the strategic management process?
   Answer – Page 95

7. What are grand strategies, and how does each shape the work of a manager?
   Answer – Pages 95-98

8. Describe Michael Porter's generic strategies, explaining the competitive advantage each brings to a company.
   Answer – Pages 97-99

9. How can quality provide a competitive advantage? Give an example.
   Answer – Pages 99-100

10. How does entrepreneurship reshape the strategic management process? How and what priorities are changed, etc.?
    Answer – Pages 103-104

STUDY QUIZ
Multiple Choice Questions
1. Planning has a number of benefits including:
   a) forcing managers to look ahead and anticipate change.
   b) enabling managers to better manage in a chaotic environment.
   c) facilitating control through objectives and standards.
   d) all of these.

2. Critics of organizational planning argue that:
   a) too few managers have training in the process to make it worthwhile.
   b) it causes managers to focus on tomorrow's survival not today's competition.
   c) it tends to reinforce failure, as managers tend to try what they know, just more of it.
   d) it is not a substitute for managers' intuition and creativity.

3. According to research on planning and organizational performance:
   a) there is little relationship between planning and high performance.
   b) where there is planning there are generally higher profits and higher return on assets.
   c) there is less innovation and creativity but better resource controls when companies plan.
   d) the format or structure of the planning process is more important than the quality of the process in generating a positive impact on the organization.

4. Education Priorities is a for-profit educational institution. One of its goals is to acquire three other learning educational companies within three years in order to become a national presence in education. Its goal is an example of a:
   a) short-term, specific goal.
   b) standing plan.
   c) tactical or operational plan.
   d) long-term, directional goal.

5. The MBO process uses goals to:
   a) motivate employees' behavior.
   b) control resources and employees.
   c) allocate organizational resources.
   d) set the strategic direction of the company.

6. When using MBOs, the first step in setting employee objectives is to:
   a) prioritize the goals.
   b) allow the employee to participate.
   c) identify key job tasks.
   d) link rewards to goal attainment.

7. The first step in the strategic management process is:
   a) formulating strategies.
   b) analyzing the environment.
   c) analyzing organizational resources.
   d) identifying the current mission, objectives, and strategies of the firm.

8. Nancy and Kim are reviewing large amounts of information from several sources trying to spot trends in their industry while creating what-if scenarios to discuss with the management team. They are in the process of:
   a) conducting a SWOT analysis.
   b) evaluating their core competencies.
   c) environmental scanning.
   d) formulating strategies.

9. Which of the following is true about the collecting of competitive intelligence?
   a) 95% of the information needed and gathered is already public.
   b) It is a necessary part of developing your company's core competencies.
   c) It is illegal in almost all states.
   d) None of these are true.

10. When managers conduct a SWOT analysis as part of the strategic planning process, they are:
    a) scanning the environment for competitive intelligence using information technology.
    b) studying their company's strengths and weaknesses and the competitive threats and market opportunities.
    c) systematically working on technology as a competitive advantage.
    d) evaluating their company's core competencies.

11. Morey is considering grand strategies for his company. He wants to serve the same market, customers with the same product and pricing. His market is relatively unchanging, and his company doesn't have any real strengths or weaknesses in its performance. His best choice would be a:
    a) retrenchment strategy.
    b) cost-leadership strategy.
    c) stability strategy.
    d) growth strategy.

12. In order to sustain its competitive advantage, a company may:
    a) use patents or trademarks to protect its products.
    b) reduce its products to increase volume and economies of scale.
    c) use exclusive contracts with its suppliers.
    d) do all or any of these.

13. If Bill Hinton is trying to improve the quality of his products by buying, analyzing, and then copying the methods used by the best competitors in his field, he is:
    a) involved in illegal competitive intelligence.
    b) using the ISO 9000 quality process.
    c) benchmarking his products.
    d) using TQM techniques.

14. The _____ quality process strives to design quality into a product while it is being made and seeks to reduce defects to less than 4 per million items produced.
    a) six sigma
    b) ISO 9000
    c) benchmarking
    d) total quality management

15. Research on the entrepreneurial personality shows that they:
    a) are independent types who plan extensively and take calculated risks.
    b) tend to be poor innovators but especially skilled at selling.
    c) are just like managers, just self-employed.
    d) tend to be young, white, and male.

True/False Questions

1. Planning, while a useful tool for coordinating effort, does little to reduce uncertainty in today's business environment.

2. Research shows that managers' intuition and creativity are more effective in stimulating and helping them focus on tomorrow's survival than formal plans are.

3. If Tim is working on a plan for how his telecommunications unit will help the company meet its organizational goals, he is creating a tactical or operational plan.

4. Directional plans are ones that set specific goals and objectives at both the unit and individual level.

5. MBO is built on four elements, the first of which is goal specificity.

6. Research shows that unless goals are set participatively in the MBO process, they will not be achieved.

7. W. Edwards Deming was an ardent supporter of MBO as the human element of his statistical control process in the implementation of TQM programs.

8. If Elmer is working on defining what business his company is in and why the company exists as part of the company's strategic planning process, Elmer is working on the first step, Mission, of the planning process.

9. The primary difference between scanning the environment for information and competitive intelligence is that scanning the environment is legal and competitive intelligence implies illegal gathering of competitive information.

10. When an executive is studying the skills and abilities of his employees, his firm's cash flow, its ability to develop new products, etc., he is conducting a threat/opportunity analysis as part of the strategic planning process.

11. A growth strategy can be accomplished through increasing sales revenues, increasing market share, by merging with another company, or acquiring another company, etc.

12. According to Michael Porter's competitive strategy, if a firm seeks to build a competitive advantage on the uniqueness of its products, technology, innovative design, etc., the firm is pursuing a cost-leadership strategy.

13. The key to a competitive advantage is its sustainability.

14. A quality competitive advantage is generally not sustainable because other companies can easily copy it.

15. ISO 9000 is actually a set of standards that assures customers that a company uses a specific process to manage its quality, it isn't an actual quality management standard.

Answers to Chapter 3 Study Quiz

Multiple Choice (Page - Answer)

1. d-81	6. c-88	11. c-96
2. d-82	7. d-90	12. d-98
3. b-83	8. c-91	13. c-100
4. d-85	9. a-92	14. a-102
5. a-86	10. b-95	15. a-104-105

True/False

1. F-81	6. F-88	11. T-95
2. F-82	7. F-89	12. F-97
3. T-84	8. T-90	13. T-98
4. F-85	9. F-92	14. F-100
5. T-86	10. F-93-94	15. T-101

CHAPTER 4 - FOUNDATIONS OF DECISION-MAKING LEARNING OUTCOMES

LEARNING OUTCOMES

After reading this chapter, you should be able to:
1. Describe the steps in the decision-making process.
2. Identify the assumptions of the rational decision making model.
3. Explain the limits to rationality.
4. Define certainty, risk, and uncertainty as they relate to decision-making.
5. Describe the actions of the bounded-rational decision maker.
6. Identify the two types of decision problems and the two types of decisions that are used to solve them.
7. Define heuristics, and explain how they affect the decision-making process.
8. Identify four decision-making styles.
9. Describe the advantages and disadvantages of group decisions.
10. Explain three techniques for improving group decision making.

Use the Outline to Guide Your Note Taking from the Text

Considerations as you read

As you read and take notes, think about these question;s they will help you organize your study notes.
1. Outline the steps of the decision making process, explaining what takes place in each step.
2. Compare and contrast the rational and bounded rationality decision-making models.
3. What is a contingency approach to decision-making and its various elements?
4. How does one's individual style affect the decision-making process?
5. When should a manager use a group to make a decision? Is their process different than an individual's?
6. What impact does national culture have on the decision-making process?

I. THE DECISION-MAKING PROCESS
A. Introduction
1. Decision making is typically described as
2. This is simplistic because decision making is
   a) See Exhibit 4-2 illustrating the decision-making process.

B. What Defines a Decision Problem?
1. The decision-making process begins with
   a) Nokia example
   b) Car-buying example
2. Problem identification is
3. The manager who mistakenly solves the wrong problem
4. How do managers
   a) Managers compare

C. What Is Relevant in the Decision-Making Process?
1. Once a problem is identified
2. Car-buying example continued.
3. Every decision maker has
   a) What is not identified is
4. If a decision maker does not

D. How Does the Decision Maker Weight the Criteria?
1. It is necessary to weight the items listed in step 2 in order to
2.
3. A simple approach,
    a) Exhibit 4-3 lists the criteria and weights for car-replacement decision.
4. The next step, list the
    a) No attempt is made to
5. Once identified, the decision maker must
    a) Each alternative is evaluated by
    b) Most decisions contain
    c) If you multiply each alternative assessment against
    d) Notice that

E. What Determines the "Best" Choice?
1. The sixth step,
    a) Car example, Exhibit 4-5.

F. What Is Decision Implementation?
1. The decision may still fail if
2. Decision implementation includes
3. The people who

G. What Is the Last Step in the Decision Process?
1. The last step (step 8)
2. Did the alternative chosen in step 6 and implemented in step 7

II. MAKING DECISIONS: THE RATIONAL MODEL
A. Introduction
1. Managerial decision making is
2. A decision maker who was
    a) Carefully defining
    b) The decision-making process would
    c) Exhibit 4-6 summarizes the
3. The assumptions of rationality often
4. Most managers try to
    a) This process is dealing with
5. Decisions made with limited information

III. THE REAL WORLD OF MANAGERIAL DECISION MAKING: MODIFICATION OF THE RATIONAL MODEL
A. Introduction
1. Most of us make decisions on the basis of
2. When we are faced with complex problems, most of us
3. Satisficing

B. Do Managers Engage in Satisficing Behavior?
1. When managers are faced with a simple problem having
2. Studies often challenge
    a) They suggest that decision making
    b) Despite the limits to perfect rationality
3. "Good" decision makers are

4. Managers signal that
   a) This is frequently referred to

C. What Is Bounded Rationality?
1. Management theory is built on the premise that
2. The essence of managerial jobs revolves around
   a) However,
3. Herbert Simon found that
4. Because it is impossible
   a) Bounded rationality,
   b) The result is

D. How Do Managers' Actions within These Boundaries Differ from Actions within the Rational Model?
1. Once a problem is identified,
   a) This list of criteria is generally
2. Simon found that decision makers focus on
3. This means developing alternatives that
4. Once this
   a) The review will
5. They review alternatives
   a) The first alternative

E. What Are the Implications of Bounded Rationality on the Manager's Job?
1. In situations in which the assumptions of perfect rationality do not apply
2.

F. Are There Common Errors Committed in the Decision-Making Process?
1. Making decisions is making choices.
2. Behaviors that speed up the process,
3. Two forms
   a) Both types
   b) Another bias,
4. Availability heuristic.
   a) The tendency for people to
   b) Example, fear of flying.
5. Representative heuristic
   a) Literally millions of recreational league players
   b) In reality
   c) Representative heuristic causes
6. Organizational instances of representative heuristic.
   a) Predicting the future success of a new product by
   b) No longer hiring
7. Escalation of commitment
   a) An
   b) The tendency to
   c) Some of the best-recorded events involving escalation of commitment were
   d) The commitment to the original solution may be

IV. DECISION MAKING: A CONTINGENCY APPROACH
A. How Do Problems Differ?
1. Some problems are straightforward
2. Many situations however, are

B. What Is the Difference between Programmed and Nonprogrammed Decisions?
1. Programmed, or routine, decision making is
2. When problems are ill-structured,
    a) A Sears Automotive mechanic example.
3. Decisions are programmed to the extent that
    a) Programmed decision making is
    b) The "develop-the-alternatives" stage is

C. What Are Procedures, Rules, and Policies, and When Are They Best Used?
1. A procedure is a series of
    a) The only real difficulty is
    b) Once the problem is clear
    c) Example of purchasing manager and request for copies of Microsoft Outlook.
2. A rule is an explicit statement that
    a) Rules are frequently
3. A policy provides guidelines to
    a) In contrast to a rule, a policy

D. What Do Nonprogrammed Decisions Look Like?
1. Examples of nonprogrammed decisions.
    a)
    b)
2. Such decisions are
3. The creation of
    a) Example, Eli Lilly & Company's decision to

E. How Can You Integrate Problems, Types of Decisions, and Level in the Organization?
1. Exhibit 4-7 describes
2. Well-structured problems are
    a) Lower-level managers essentially
3. Ill-structured problems require
    a) The problems confronting managers up
4. Few managerial decisions are
5. Organizational efficiency is facilitated by the use of
    a) Whenever possible, management decisions are
    b) There are strong economic incentives
    c) Programmed decisions
    d) This benefit is important because

V. DECISION-MAKING STYLES
A. Introduction
1. Every decision maker
2. Research has sought to identify

B. The Model
1. The basic premise is that

2. The first is the way they
    a) Some decision makers are
    b) Some individuals who
3. The second dimension focuses on
    a) Some have a high need for
    b) Others tolerate
4. When we diagram these two dimensions,
    a) These styles are
    b) See Exhibit 4-8.
5. The directive style.
    a) Represents a decision-making style characterized by
    b) These individuals are
6. The analytic style.
    a) Characterized by
    b) These individuals prefer
7. The conceptual style
    a) Tends to be
    b) Tends to focus on
8. The behavioral style
    a) Reflects an individual who
    b) These decision makers work well with
9. Most managers possess characteristics of more than one style.
    a) See the Self-Assessment exercise.

VI. MAKING DECISIONS IN GROUPS
A. Do Managers Make a Lot of Decisions in Groups?
1. Many decisions in organizations, especially important decisions
2. In many cases, these groups represent
3. Managers spend up to

B. What Are the Advantages to Group Decision Making?
1. Individual and group decisions have their own set of strengths.
2. Group decisions provide
3. A group will
4. Groups also
    a)
    b)
5. Group decision making
6. This process increases

C. What Are the Disadvantages to Group Decision Making?
1. First, they are
2. There may also be
    a) Members of a group
    b) A minority that
3. Another problem focuses on
    a) There are
    b) Irving Janis'
4. Finally, there is
5. Groupthink applies to
    a) Because of pressures for

    b) Consequently, there is
6. How does groupthink occur?
    a) Group members
    b) Members apply
    c) Those members who have doubts
    d) There is an illusion of
7. Does groupthink really hinder decision making?
    a)
8. But, groupthink can be minimized if:
    a)
    b)
    c)

D. When Are Groups Most Effective?
1. On the average, groups
2. If decision effectiveness is defined
3. If creativity is important,
4. If effectiveness means
5. The effectiveness is also influenced by
    a) The larger the group,
    b) But,
    c) A minimum of
    d) Because
6. Effectiveness should not be considered
    a) Groups almost

E. How Can You Improve Group Decision Making?
1. Three ways of making group decision
2. What is brainstorming?
    a) A relatively
    b) It utilizes
    c) Brainstorming is
3. How does the nominal group technique work?
    a) The technique
    b) Group members must
    c) They
    d) The chief advantage is
4. How can electronic meetings enhance group decision making?
    a) This approach blends
    b) Once the technology
    c) Up to
    d) Issues are
    e) Individual comments
    f) The major advantages of electronic meetings are
5. Experts claim that
    a) Phelps Dodge Mining example.
6. Drawbacks
    a) Those who can
    b) Those with
    c) The process lacks
7. But this technology

8. A variation of the electronic meeting is
   a) By linking together media from different locations
   b) This has enhanced

VII. NATIONAL CULTURE AND DECISION-MAKING PRACTICES
A. Introduction
1. Research shows that,
2. Two decision variables.
   a)
   b)
3. India,
   a) There only
4. Sweden,
   a) Swedish senior managers
5. Egypt,
   a)
6. Italy,
   a)
7. Decision making in Japan is
   a) The Japanese value
   b) Japanese CEOs
   c) Managerial decisions
8. France,
9. Managerial styles in Germany reflect

VIII. DECISION MAKING FROM A CROSS-DISCIPLINARY PERSPECTIVE
A. How Humanities and Social Science Disciplines Influence a Manager's Thinking
1. In economics,
   a) Business decision makers who
2. Psychology is helpful in
   a) Bounded rationality,
   b) And much of what we know about
3. Political science.
   a) How these elements affect
4. Philosophies
   a) Philosophy helps develop

REVIEW QUESTIONS
1. Explain how decision making is related to the planning process.
   Answer – Pages 114-115

2. Outline the rational decision-making process, naming and explaining each step.
   Answer – Pages 115-119

3. What are the underlying assumptions of the rational decision model?
   Answer – Page 119

4. How do certainty, risk, and uncertainty affect individuals when they make a decision? How does escalation of commitment affect decision making?
   Answer – Page 119

5. What is bounded rationality and how does it improve on the rational decision-making model?
   Answer – Pages 120-121

6. What is the role of heuristics in bounded rationality?
   Answer – Pages 122-123

7. What are programmed and nonprogrammed decisions, and what is the relationship of management level to these two classes of decisions?
   Answer – Pages 124-126

8. Review the four major decision-making styles, describing each and their strengths and weaknesses.
   Answer – Pages 127-127

9. When should a manager use a group to make a decision? What are the strengths and weaknesses of group decision making?
   Answer – Page 129

10. List the various techniques that can be used to improve group decision making noting what weaknesses each technique overcomes.
    Answer – Pages 131-132

11. How does national culture affect managerial decision making?
    Answer – Pages 132-133

STUDY QUIZ
Multiple Choice Questions

1. Malcolm is trying to figure out why his lead sales professional's sales productivity has dropped so dramatically over the last quarter. In terms of decision making and problem solving Malcolm's first step should be to:
   a) define his problem.
   b) determine criteria for making a decision.
   c) develop possible alternative ways to solve the problem.
   d) analyze the problem and alternatives for solving it.

2. Joni is trying to decide what is most important to her in the performance of her employees as she reviews her list of behaviors in the development of a performance appraisal instrument. In terms of decision making, Joni is at:
   a) stage 4, listing the various alternative behaviors she could see in her employees.
   b) stage 3, prioritizing or weighting her decision criteria.
   c) stage 2, choosing her basic criteria.
   d) stage 1, identifying what her problem is.

3. The actual analysis of the strengths and weaknesses of the choices available to use in making a decision actually comes:
   a) at the very beginning of the process.
   b) at the very end of the decision process.
   c) after choosing alternatives but before choosing the best alternative.
   d) before prioritizing or weighting the alternatives but after choosing the basic criteria for deciding.

4. In the traditional rational decision-making model, when a manager has to make a decision with a limited amount of information and cannot assess the probability of the outcomes, he/she is dealing with:
   a) bounded rationality.
   b) a satisficing decision.
   c) the condition of uncertainty.
   d) an ineffective alternative set.

5. The bounded rationality decision making model argues that:
   a) most problems are clear and unambiguous.
   b) decision makers use simplified models in deciding.
   c) managers' preferences as to choice is almost always clear.
   d) the final choice made will be made to maximize the economic payoff for the firm.

6. Cheng is concerned about passing his business calculus final. His grades have been steadily dropping on each successive test in this class, and the professor has a reputation for a 50% failure rate. He's talked with the professor and she was not helpful. Cheng decides to drop the class and retake it under another professor. Cheng most likely used _____ in making his decision.
   a) an availability heuristic
   b) the escalation of commitment
   c) a representative heuristic
   d) a quarter that he tossed in the air

7. Which of the following is an example of a programmed decision?
   a) A firm is deciding whether or not to begin an e-commerce web site.
   b) A company decides to hire an external candidate in violation of its standard policy to promote from within.
   c) The secretary orders office supplies from their regular supplier when they are low, up to a set dollar cost.
   d) A college student takes an interest inventory and then chooses a major on the basis of the instrument's feedback.

8. A _____ is an explicit statement that tells a manager what he/she should or should not do in a given situation.
   a) procedure
   b) rule
   c) policy
   d) standing plan

9. Generally speaking, when considering the relationship of type of problem, type of decision, and level within the organization of the decision maker, it is safe to say that:
   a) the higher in an organization a manager is, the more well-structured problems he/she will face.
   b) the lower in an organization a manager is, the more programmed decisions he/she will make.
   c) middle-level managers face more ill-structured problems, make make more programmed decisions than lower level managers.
   d) the lower the level in the organization, the fewer nonprogrammed decisions a manager faces.

10. Alison has a broad outlook on problems and wants as many alternatives as possible. She is concerned about the long run and looks for creative solutions. Alison's decision style is most likely to be:
    a) directive.
    b) analytical.
    c) conceptual.
    d) behavioral.

11. Group-based decisions have a number of advantages of individually made decisions, such as:
    a) they take less time because they consider fewer alternatives.
    b) they tend to be of better quality.
    c) they are more predictable and less creative.
    d) being more rational and less subject to organizational politics.

12. Group decision making also has a number of disadvantages including:
    a) no one person being accountable or responsible for the decision.
    b) their tendency to adopt satisfacing behavior in order to reach a consensus.
    c) less acceptance by those affected due to the compromises inherent in the group process.
    d) poor implementation record by management.

13. Why does group think happen?
    a) Group members rationalize any resistance away.
    b) Those who deviate from the common solution discredit themselves.
    c) The group forms a desire to please the leader, damping resistance.
    d) Brainstorming is done incorrectly.

14. If you strive to improve your group's decision making by reducing the pressure to conform and striving to generate as many alternative choices as possible, but need to work face-to-face, your best choice of group decision technique would be:
    a) nominal group technique.
    b) the Delphi technique.
    c) an electronic meeting.
    d) brainstorming.

15. When making decisions in other countries, research shows that:
    a) power distance and uncertainty avoidance have little impact on decision-making practices.
    b) the perception of time pressures or lack thereof surprisingly does not influence decision making all that much.
    c) the decision-making process and styles found in the United States are also universally found in other countries.
    d) when power distance and uncertainty avoidance are low, decision making tends to be pushed down to the lowest levels possible.

True/False Questions

1. If Jessie is trying to decide whether price, durability, or style should be considered in the purchase of her summer wardrobe she is most likely at step 4, choosing alternatives in the decision process.

2. The last step in the decision process, prior to implementation of the decision, is choosing the best alternative from those listed and evaluated.

3. The rational decision-making model assumes that most decisions work from a single, well-defined goal.

4. Satisficing in bounded rationality is the process of choosing the alternative that will satisfy the largest number of stakeholders.

5. When Bethany keeps putting money into her 401(k) plan even though the stock it holds continues to go down, because she's invested this long she might as well see it through, Bethany is exhibiting the use of a representative heuristic in her decision.

6. When a manager decides to keep a product development project going, even when he/she knows it will fail, simply because the company has already invested so much into the project, he/she is demonstrating the principle, escalation of commitment.

7. Policies, procedures, rules, etc., are all tools that assist managers when they make programmed decisions.

8. If a decision is unique and nonrecurring, such as trying to decide whether to modify a product or introduce a whole new product, the manager is facing a nonprogrammed decision.

9. The model of decision making styles used in the text, divides individuals into four categories based on their tolerance for ambiguity and they way they think.

10. When it comes to decision-making styles, most managers do not have a dominate style.

11. It is possible that a group-based decision could be of poor quality if the group experiences minority domination.

12. Groupthink, while well-documented, really has little effect on the quality of decisions a group makes but it does have a large impact on the way a decision is implemented.

13. The most effective groups are larger 12-18 and are even-numbered to force groups to create a majority for a decision, because a split vote immobilizes the group.

14. Research shows that electronic meetings are faster than traditional meetings but the lack of informational richness of face-to-face meetings may result in "good typists" dominating the meeting.

15. There are few significant differences in decision-making practices among different cultures because the decision-making model is American and has permeated almost all countries.

Answers to Chapter 4 Study Quiz

Multiple Choice (Page - Answer)

1. a-115	6. a-122	11. b-129
2. b-116	7. c-124	12. a-129
3. c-118	8. b-125	13. a-130
4. c-119	9. d-126	14. d-131
5. b-131	10. c-128	15. d-132

True/False

1. F-115	6. T-123	11. T-129
2. T-118	7. T-124	12. F-130
3. T-119	8. T-126	13. F-131
4. F-121	9. T-127	14. T-131
5. F-122	10. F-128	15. F-132

QUANTITATIVE MODULE
QUANTITATIVE DECISION-MAKING AIDS

Use the Outline to Guide Your Note Taking from the Text

Considerations as You Read

As you read and take notes, think about these questions; they will help you organize your study notes.
1. Create a chart outlining the benefits and weaknesses of each type of decision tool.
2. In what circumstances would each of the decision tools best fit?
3. Why is business so enamored with quantitative decision-making tools?

I. INTRODUCTION
A. Decision-Making Aids and Techniques
    1. Payoff matrices,
    2. The purpose of each of these methods is

II. PAYOFF MATRICES
A. Factors Affecting Decisions
    1. Uncertainty
    2. Another factor,
        a) An optimistic manager follows
        b) The pessimist will pursue
        c) The manager who desires to minimize his "regret" will opt for
    3. Example of a marketing manager at Discover International in New York.
        a) Four possible strategies,
        b) His major competitor, Visa, has
        c) The Discover card manager formulates the matrix.
    4. If our Discover manager is an optimist, he'll
    5. If our manager is a pessimist, he
    6. Third, there may be a regret of profits
    7. Managers calculate regret by
        a) See Exhibit QM-2.
    8. Our Discover-manager would choose

III. DECISION TREES
    1. Decision trees are
        a) When diagrammed, they
        b) Typical decision trees encompass
    2. Exhibit QM-3 illustrates one decision.
        a) Mike Rosenthal and
        b) Mike's group
        c)
        d)
        e)
        f) Exhibit QM-3, shows the decision elements.

IV. BREAK-EVEN ANALYSIS
1. Break-even analysis is
2. Break-even analysis is
   a) It points out the relationship among
   b) To compute the break-even point
3. An organization breaks even when
   a) Fixed costs are
   b) Variable costs
4. The break-even point can be computed graphically or by using the following formula:

$$ = \overline{} $$

   a) This formula tells us that
5. The usefulness of break-even is shown graphically in Exhibit QM-4.
6. As a planning tool, break-even analysis

V. RATIO ANALYSIS
1. An organization's financial documents can
2. Managers often analyze key ratios
3. The more useful ratios evaluate
   a) Summarized in Exhibit QM-5.
4. What are liquidity ratios?
   a) Liquidity is a measure of
   b) The most popular are
   c) The current ratio is
   d) The acid test ratio is
   e) Accountants typically consider an
5. Leverage ratios refer to
   a) The advantage of leverage
   b) There are risks to over-leveraging.
   c) Leverage ratios such as
6. Operating-ratios describe
   a) The most popular are
   b) The inventory turnover ratio is
      (1)
   c) Total assets turnover ratio
      (1) It measures
      (2) The fewer assets used
7. Profitability ratios enable
   a) The better known of these are
   b) The profit-margin-on-revenues ratio
   c) One of the most widely used, return-on-investment ratio, is

VI. LINEAR PROGRAMMING
1. Natalie Lopez's software development company
2. She can use
   a) Linear programming cannot
   b) It requires
   c) There must also be

3. Many different types of problems can be solved using linear programming.
   a)
   b)
   c)
4. For complex linear programming problems, there is
5. See Exhibits QM-6 and MM-7 for its application to Natalie's business.

VII. QUEUING THEORY
1. Branch bank cashier stations example.
2. Queuing theory,
3. Whenever a decision involves
   a)
   b)
   c)
   d) In each situation, management wants to
4. The mathematics underlying queuing theory is beyond the scope of this book.
5. But you can see how the theory works in a simple example.

$$P_n = 1 - \frac{\text{arrival rate}}{\text{service rate}} \quad X \quad \frac{\text{arrival rate}}{\text{service rate}}^n$$

VIII. ECONOMIC ORDER QUANTITY MODEL
1. One of the
   a) See Exhibit QM-8.
2. The EOQ model seeks to
   a) When these four costs are known
3. The objective of the economic order quantity (EOQ) model is
4. As the amount ordered gets larger
5. The most economic order quantity is reached at
6. That's the point at which
   a) See point Q in Exhibit QM-8.
7. The inventory model suggests to Sam that
8. These calculations suggest to Sam that
9. A word of caution.
   a) The EOQ model assumes that
   b) If these conditions can't be met
10. The mathematics for EOQ, like queuing theory, go far beyond the scope of this text!

REVIEW QUESTIONS
1. What is the value of a payoff matrix for managers?
   Answer – Page 142

2. Take a simple decision, choosing a new car, and diagram it on a decision tree.
   Answer – Pages 142-143

3. What is ratio analysis? Create a chart of the various ratios, noting their formulas, and what each helps a manager to track.
   Answer – Pages 144-146

4. What is linear programming, and when would a manager use it?
   Answer – Pages 147-148

5. How do managers calculate and use EOQ?
   Answer – Pages 149-150

STUDY QUIZ
Multiple Choice Questions

1. A manager who wishes to minimize his/her "regret of profits" will most likely make a payoff choice:
   a) that would produce the maximum gain.
   b) that would maximize the minimum possible gain.
   c) that would minimize the maximum possible loss.
   d) that would minimize the profits forgone due to another course of action.

2. When managers need to make a series of decisions, each of which builds on a previous decision the most useful tool to analyze the decisions is a:
   a) decision tree.
   b) payoff matrix.
   c) linear progress.
   d) break-even analysis.

3. A break-even analysis is represented by which of the following formulas?

   a) $P_n = 1 - \dfrac{\text{arrival rate}}{\text{service rate}} \times \dfrac{\text{arrival rate}}{\text{service rate}}^n$

   b) $BE = \dfrac{TFC}{P\text{-}VC}$

   c) $TIE = \dfrac{P_b\,I + T}{\text{Total Int. Charges}}$

   d) None of these.

4. The _____ tells the manager how much volume has to increase to make a profit or how much volume he/she can afford to lose and still make a profit.
   a) current ratio
   b) payoff matrix
   c) leverage ratio
   d) break-even analysis

5. The acid test:
   a) more accurately measures liquidity when inventory turnover is slow or inventory is difficult to sell.
   b) measures the efficiency of assets in generating profit.
   c) tests the organization's ability to meet short-term debt.
   d) measures how far the decline in profits can go before bankruptcy.

6. The profitability ratio that measures profit per dollar of revenue is:
   a) profits before interest and taxes/total interest charges.
   b) net profit after taxes/total revenues.
   c) current assets/current liabilities.
   d) net profit after taxes/total assets.

7. The quantitative analytical tool that requires that a change in one variable will be accompanied by a proportional change in another variable, in order to be effective is:
   a) ratio analysis.
   b) queuing theory.
   c) linear programming.
   d) economic order quantity model.

8. Queuing theory is best represented by which of the following formulas?

   a) $P_n = 1 - \dfrac{\text{arrival rate}}{\text{service rate}} \times \dfrac{\text{arrival rate}}{\text{service rate}}^n$

   b) $BE = \dfrac{TFC}{P\text{-}VC}$

   c) $TIE = \dfrac{P_b\, I + T}{\text{Total Int. Charges}}$

   d) $EOQ = \dfrac{2 \times D \times OC}{V \times CC}$

9. _____ takes into consideration forecasted product demand, order costs, value of the product, and carrying costs of inventory.
   a) ratio analysis.
   b) queuing theory.
   c) linear programming.
   d) economic order quantity model.

10. The economic order quantity model assumes that:
    a) demand and lead time is known and constant.
    b) products will be ordered at the lowest per-item cost possible.
    c) current inventory has not yet been depleted.
    d) there is a point of maximum profits.

True/False Questions

1. Aside from the amount of information available, there is evidence that a manager's psychological orientation, optimist or pessimist, affects his/her decisions.

2. In a payoff matrix, the "regret of profits," refers to managerial concern for the ethicality of the decision made when inappropriate means are used to maximize the outcome of the decision.

3. A payoff matrix is a decision tool that allows managers to assign probabilities to each possible outcome and calculate the payoffs for each decision path.

4. The break-even analysis is a statistical tool that allows managers to review the relationships between revenues, costs, and profits.

5. The ability of a firm to meet its financial obligation may be analyzed through the use of profit ratio.

6. With the inventory turnover ratio, the lower the ratio, the more turnover there is of inventory.

7. To be effective as an analytical tool, linear programming requires limited resources, the objectives of the organization, and alternatives for combining resources to produce a particular output.

8. Queuing theory is used in manufacturing to develop the most efficient process for making goods by analyzing the order of the steps in the production process.

9. When managers wish to determine the best time to order inventory as they seek to balance purchase costs, ordering costs, carrying costs, and stockout costs they should use a total asset turnover model.

10. The objective of the economic order quantity model is to minimize total costs associated with carrying inventory.

Answers to Chapter 4a Study Quiz

Multiple Choice (Page - Answer)

1. d-142	6. b-146
2. a-144	7. c-147
3. b-144	8. a-149
4. d-144	9. d-149
5. a-145	10. b-150

True/False

1. T-141-2	6. F-146
2. F-142	7. T-147
3. F-143	8. F-149
4. T-144	9. F-149
5. F145	10. T-149

PART 3: ORGANIZING
CHAPTER 5 - BASIC ORGANIZATION DESIGNS

LEARNING OUTCOMES

After reading this chapter, you should be able to:
1. Identify and define the six elements of organization structure.
2. Describe the advantages and disadvantages of work specialization.
3. Contrast authority and power.
4. Identify the five different ways by which management can departmentalize.
5. Contrast mechanistic and organic organizations.
6. Summarize the effect on organization structures of strategy, size, technology, and environment.
7. Contrast the divisional and functional structures.
8. Explain the strengths of the matrix structure.
9. Describe the boundaryless organization and what elements have contributed to its development.
10. Describe what is meant by the term *organization culture*.

Use the Outline to Guide Your Note Taking from the Text

Considerations as you read

As you read and take note, think about these questions; they will help you organize your study notes.
1. What are the various elements of organizational structure, and how does each influence an organization's structure?
2. Compare and contrast the mechanistic and organic structures.
3. Create a chart showing the types of organizational structure, and identify under what circumstances the structure is most effective.
4. What is organizational culture? What is its relationship to organizational structure?

I. **INTRODUCTION**
   A. **The Steve Siegel Example**
      1. Demonstrates the importance of
      2. Once decisions regarding corporate strategies are made
         a) When managers develop or change the organization's structure, they
      3. Organization design decisions are
      4. Organization design applies to

II. **THE ELEMENTS OF STRUCTURE**
   A. **The Basic Concepts of Organization Design**
      1. Formulated by management writers in the early years of this century.
      2. These principles still provide

   B. **What Is Work Specialization?**
      1. In the 1700s, Adam Smith
      2. A job is
         a) Individuals
         b) Work specialization makes
      3. Some tasks require

C. What Is the Chain of Command?
1. The early management writers argued
2. If the chain of command had to be violated
3. The chain of command concept was

D. What Is the Span of Control?
1. How many employees can a manager efficiently and effectively direct?
2. This question received
3. There was
4. Level in the organization is
   a) Top managers need
5. There is some change
6. Many organizations are
   a) The span for managers has
7. The span of control is
   a) The more
8. Other contingency variables

E. What Are Authority and Responsibility?
1. Authority refers to
2. Authority was
   a) It was to be
3. Each management position has
   a) Authority is
4. When a position of authority is vacated
5. When managers delegate authority, they
   a) Allocating authority
   b) No one should be

F. Are There Different Types of Authority Relationships?
1. The early management writers distinguished between two forms of authority.
   a)
   b)
   c) A manager's function is
2. As organizations get larger and more complex
   a) They create
   b) Exhibit 5-3 illustrates

G. How Does the Contemporary View of Authority and Responsibility Differ from the Historical View?
1. The early management writers actively
2. This might have been true
3. It is now recognized that you
4. Authority is but one element

H. How Do Authority and Power Differ?
1. Authority and power are frequently
2. Authority is
   a) Authority goes

   3. Power refers to
      a) Authority is
      b) Exhibit 5-4
   4. Power is
      a) It includes not
      b) While authority is
   5. Think of the cone in Exhibit 5-4.
      a) The closer you are to the power core
      b) The existence of a power core
   6. The cone analogy explicitly
      a) The higher one moves in an organization
   7. It is not necessary to
      a) Example, administrative assistants,
      b) Low-ranking employees
      c) So, too, are employees with
         (1) The lowly production engineer
   8. Power can come from different areas.
      a) John French and Bertram Raven have identified
         (1) Summarized them in

I. How Do Centralization and Decentralization Differ?
   1. Centralization is a function of
   2. Centralization-decentralization is
   3. By that we mean that no organization is
   4. Early management writers felt that
      a) Their objective was
      b) Traditional organizations were
      c) Given this structure,
   5. Organizations today are
      a) Many managers believe that
   6. Today, managers often choose
   7. One of the central themes of empowering employees was
      a) That's decentralization at work!
      b) However, that it doesn't imply that

J. Can You Identify the Five Ways to Departmentalize?
   1. Early management writers argued that
   2. Work specialization creates
      a) This is facilitated by
   3. Creation of these departments is
   4. No single method of departmentalization was

K. How Are Activities Grouped?
   1. One of the most popular ways to group activities is by
      a) See Exhibit 5-6.
      b) Functional departmentalization can

2. Exhibit 5-7 illustrates
   a) Each major product area in the corporation is
   b) Another company that
      (1) Its structure is
   c) Service-related organization's activities
      (1) For instance, an accounting firm.
3. The particular type of customer
4. See Exhibit 5-8.
   a) The assumption is that
5. Another way to departmentalize is
   a) See Exhibit 5-9.
   b) Valuable, if an organization's customers are
6. Process departmentalization,
   a) Exhibit 5-10 represents
   b) If you have ever been to a state motor vehicle office

L. **How Does the Contemporary View of Departmentalization Differ from the Historical View?**
   1. Most large organizations
   2. Recently however, rigid departmentalization is being
      a) Today's competitive environment has
   3. To better monitor the needs of customers
      a) The Dana Corporation, for example.
   4. As tasks have become more
   5. Early writers believed the ideal
   6. Today, we recognize that there is

III. CONTINGENCY VARIABLES AFFECTING STRUCTURE
A. Introduction
   1. The most appropriate structure to use
   2. The more popular contingency variables

B. How Is a Mechanistic Organization Different from an Organic Organization?
   1. Exhibit 5-11 describes two organizational forms.
   2. The mechanistic organization
      a) The chain of command principle
      b) Keeping the span of control
      c) The high degree of division of labor
      d) Departmentalization
   3. The organic form is
      a) The adhocracy's
      b) The organic organization is
   4. When each of these two models is

C. How Does Strategy Affect Structure?
   1. An organization's structure is
      a) Strategy and structure
   2. Accordingly, organizational structure should
   3. The first important research on the strategy-structure relationship was
   4. After studying organizations over a period of fifty years
      a) Organizations usually begin
      b) The simplicity of the strategy requires

      c) Decisions can be centralized
      d) As organizations grow
   5. Research has generally
      a) Organizations pursuing
      b) A cost-leadership strategy seeks

D. How Does Size Affect Structure?
   1. There is historical evidence that
   2. Large organizations
   3. The relationship is not linear

E. How Does Technology Affect Structure?
   1. Every organization uses some form of
   2. To attain its objectives
   3. Joan Woodward found that
      a) The effectiveness of organizations
   4. Most studies focused on the processes
      a) The more routine the technology,
   5. Technology that is more nonroutine

F. How Does Environment Affect Structure?
   1. Mechanistic organizations are
   2. Organic organizations are
   3. The environment-structure relationship is
   4. Global competition, accelerated product innovation,
   5. Mechanistic organizations tend to be

IV. ORGANIZATION DESIGN APPLICATIONS
  A. What Is a Simple Structure?
   1. Most organizations start as
   2. This design reflects
   3. Work specialization is
   4. The simple structure is
   5. The simple structure is
   6. The strengths of the simple structure,
      a) It is
   7. Major weaknesses
      a) It is effective
      b) It becomes increasingly
      c) As size increases,
      d) Everything depends on

  B. What Do We Mean by a Bureaucracy?
   1. Many organizations do not
   2. As the number of employees rises,
   3. Rules and regulations are implemented,
   4. At this point, a bureaucracy is formed.
   5. Two of the most popular bureaucratic design options

C. Why Do Companies Implement Functional Structures?
1. We introduced
2. The functional structure
3. Displayed in Exhibit 5-6.
4. The strength of the
   a) Economies of scale
5. The weakness of the functional structure is

D. What Is the Divisional Structure?
1. The divisional structure is
2. Hershey Foods and PepsiCo are examples.
   a) See Exhibit 5-7.
3. Each division is
   a) Central headquarters provides
   b) Headquarters acts as
4. The chief advantage of the divisional structure is
   a) Division managers have full responsibility
   b) It also frees the headquarters from
5. The major disadvantage of the divisional structure is
   a)

E. Can an Organization Design Capture the Advantages of Bureaucracies while Eliminating Their Disadvantages?
1. The functional structure offers
2. The divisional structure has
3. The matrix structure combines
   a) Exhibit 5-12 illustrates
4. The unique characteristic of the matrix is
   a) Project managers have authority over
5. Authority is shared
   a) Typically, the project manager is
   b) Decisions such as
6. To work effectively,
7. The primary strength of the matrix is that
8. The major disadvantages of the matrix lie

F. What Are Team-Based Structures?
1. The entire organization consists of
2. Team members have
3. How can team structures benefit the organization is exemplified
   a) Thermos's bureaucracy was
   b) Thermos's CEO, Monte Peterson, attacked
   c) The prime directive was
4. Since the company moved

G. Why Is There Movement toward a Boundaryless Organization?
1. A boundaryless organization is
2. It blurs the historical boundaries around
   a) Sometimes called
   b) Boundaryless structures

3. Boundaryless organizations are
   a) To do this frequently requires
   b) Horizontal organizations require
4. What factors have contributed
   a) Globalization of
   b) An organization's
   c) Changes in technology
   d) A rapidly changing environment
5. A boundaryless organization provides

V. ORGANIZATION CULTURE

A. What Is an Organization Culture?
1. A system of shared meaning.
2. Organizations have cultures that
3. Systems or patterns of values,
4. These shared values

B. How Can Cultures Be Assessed?
1. Currently there is
2. Cultures can be
   a) These characteristics are covered in Exhibit 5-13.
   b) These ten characteristics are

C. Where Does an Organization's Culture Come from?
1. An organization's culture usually reflects
   a) The founders also have
   b) They are unconstrained
   c) The small size of most new organizations
2. An organization's culture,
   a)
   b)

D. How Does Culture Influence Structure?
1. An organization's culture
2. Organizations that have a strong culture
   a) The organization's culture
   b) Strong cultures can create
3. The stronger an organization's culture

REVIEW QUESTIONS

1. What is organization design? Why is it important for managers to understand this concept?
   Answer – Page 155

2. List and explain each element of structure.
   Answer – Pages 155-166

3. How are authority and organization structure related? Authority and power?
   Answer – Pages 158-162

4. In what ways can management departmentalize? When should one method be considered over the others?
   Answer – Pages 163-166

5. Contrast mechanistic and organic structural organizational forms.
   Answer – Pages 166-167

6. What are the effects of size, environment, and technology on organizational structure?
   Answer – Pages 167-169

7. Outline the various organizational design applications noting the key characteristics and strengths of each.
   Answer – Pages 169-173

8. Describe the characteristics of a boundaryless organization structure. What is the source of an organization's culture?
   Answer – Page 173

9. What is organizational culture, from where does it originate, and how does it influence structure?
   Answer – Pages 174-176

STUDY QUIZ
Multiple Choice Questions

1. In the opening vignette, it seems that Steve Siegel took LLG from a _____ departmentalization to a _____ structure.
   a) functional; boundaryless mechanistic
   b) geographic, simple mechanistic
   c) product; team-based organic
   d) customer; matrix organic

2. Billy Bob and Janette Jean are in the process of restructuring their home improvement business from a simple to matrix and from a mechanistic to an organic organizational structure. They are involved in the task of:
   a) eliminating the chain of command.
   b) creating a functional organizational structure.
   c) work specialization.
   d) organizational design.

3. Which of the following is true about work specialization?
   a) It is a job enrichment technique designed to improve workers' satisfaction.
   b) It eventually reaches a point of diseconomy due to boredom.
   c) For most managers, it is a means of almost infinite productivity improvement.
   d) The technique requires the increasing of autonomy, task significance, and task importance.

4. Tom, first line supervisor, reports to Bill, manager, who reports to Mary, VP of Finance, who reports to Joe, the CEO. This is an example of the organizational design concept of:
   a) chain of command.
   b) span of control.
   c) matrix structure.
   d) authority.

5. _____ refers to the rights inherent in a managerial position to give orders and expect compliance.
   a) Responsibility
   b) Power
   c) Authority
   d) Staff management

6. The development of staff positions in companies came about because of:
   a) union organizing activity forcing managers to develop staff positions.
   b) increasing organizational complexity and the need to reduce line managers' work loads.
   c) the use of matrix and boundaryless organizational structures eliminating clear lines of authority.
   d) all of these.

7. Early management writers' perspective on authority and responsibility was that:
   a) authority was the same as influence in organizations.
   b) authority was simply one of several elements of power.
   c) power did not necessarily correlate with position.
   d) power and authority were not synonymous.

8. As an employee, you want to increase the amount of power you have in your company. In terms of the "cone of authority versus power," the most effective way to do that would be to:
   a) get a promotion to a higher level job.
   b) move closer to the power core.
   c) gain authority.
   d) do any of these.

9. If a manager has power due to his/her position within the organization, then his/her power is:
   a) legitimate power.
   b) referent power.
   c) reward power.
   d) expert power.

10. An internet service provider (ISP) company is organized around first-time users, academic users, business and professional users, and family users. This ISP is using a:
    a) product departmentalization.
    b) customer departmentalization.
    c) functional departmentalization.
    d) geographic departmentalization.

11. A large firm is in a rapidly changing industry, its employees are highly trained professionals, and their jobs are fairly diverse and nonroutine. The best organizational structure for this firm would be:
    a) mechanistic.
    b) organic.
    c) simple.
    d) matrix.

12. When it comes to organizational size and strategy and their relationship to organizational structure, research shows that:
    a) neither element has much of any impact on structure with high technology companies.
    b) size has little impact on structure but strategy usually forces companies to adopt boundaryless structures.
    c) size has a significant impact and strategy and structure should be matched more best effect.
    d) strategy is the number one influence on structure, with size being much less important

13. If a firm is using a product or functional departmentatization, levels of management are added to coordinate activity, informal rules give way to formal policies and procedures, the firm most likely has a:
    a) boundaryless structure.
    b) team-based structure.
    c) matrix structure.
    d) bureaucratic structure.

14. In a ____ structure there is no rigid chain of command, team members can make decisions on matters that affect them, and the organization's work is accomplished by work groups.
    a) boundaryless
    b) team-based
    c) matrix
    d) bureaucracy

15. You are evaluating a company you are considering as an employer. You are examining how much current employees identify with the company rather than their own careers or professional discipline and to what degree employees are encouraged to be aggressive, innovative, and risk-seeking. You are evaluating the company's culture in terms of:
    a) control.
    b) people focus.
    c) means-ends orientation.
    d) member identity and risk tolerance.

True/False Questions

1. Organizational design decisions are best made participatively, using input from all levels of management.

2. Managers use work specialization in order to increase the diversity of job skills needed in any one job in order to enrich the job and improve worker job satisfaction.

3. Bill has six first-line supervisors reporting to him. He is responsible for directing their work and helping them manage their subordinates. Bill's oversight of the supervisors is an example of the concept of span of control.

4. A staff manager can also have line responsibilities in the same job in the same company.

5. An individual's ability to influence decisions within an organization defines that individual's authority within the organization.

6. Early management writers wrote that the amount of centralization of decision making in an organization was a contingency variable or could vary from company to company based on the situation.

7. If your college is structured by undergraduate programs, adult learning programs, distance-learning programs, and graduate programs, it is using a geographic departmentalization.

8. If a firm has a high degree of job specialization, standardized processes, and a relatively stable business environment, it will be best served by a matrix organizational structure.

9. Research on organizational structure and strategy showed the surprising results that as companies grow in size their strategies actually become more simple and less elaborate, lending themselves to organic structures.

10. Joan Woodward's work on technology and structure showed that the most effective companies do have a strong correlation between their size of production runs and the structure of the firm.

11. A simple structure permits maximum flexibility, it is inexpensive to maintain, and provides clear accountability. Unfortunately, it does not work well in large organizations.

12. An important drawback of a divisional structure is the duplication of activities and resources within the various divisions.

13. A matrix organization and a boundaryless organization are basically the same type of structure.

14. Like a simple structure, the boundaryless organizational structure provides flexibility and fluidity facilitating quick change in order to capitalize on opportunities and respond to challenges.

15. The influence of an organization's culture on its structure depends largely on how strong the culture is.

Answers to Chapter 5 Study Quiz

Multiple Choice (Page - Answer)

1. c-154	6. b-159	11. b-167
2. d-155	7. a-159	12. c-168
3. b-154	8. d-161	13. d-170
4. a-156	9. a-162	14. b-172
5. c-158	10. b-164	15. d-174-175

True/False

1. F-155	6. T-163	11. T-169
2. F-155-156	7. F-164	12. T-170
3. T-157	8. F-166	13. F-171-173
4. T-158	9. F-168	14. T-173
5. F-160	10. T-168	15. T-175-176

CHAPTER 6 - STAFFING AND HUMAN RESOURCE MANAGEMENT

LEARNING OUTCOMES
After reading this chapter, you should be able to:
1. Describe the human resource management process.
2. Identify the influence of government regulations on human resource decisions.
3. Differentiate between job descriptions and job specifications.
4. Contrast recruitment and downsizing options.
5. Explain the importance of validity and reliability in selection.
6. Describe the selection devices that work best with various kinds of jobs.
7. Identify various training methods.
8. Explain the various techniques managers can use in evaluating employee performance.
9. Describe the goals of compensation administration and factors that affect wage structures.
10. Explain what is meant by the terms *sexual harassment, family-friendly benefits, labor-management cooperation, workplace violence,* and *layoff-survivor sickness.*

Use the Outline to Guide Your Note Taking from the Text

Considerations as you read

As you read and take notes, think about these questions; they will help you organize your study notes.
1. What legal protections do employees have in terms of human resource law?
2. What are the key elements of a human resource inventory?
3. Why would a manager choose one recruiting source over another?
4. Create a table of the selection methods showing their strengths and weaknesses.
5. Outline a performance management system and what to do if performance doesn't meet standards.
6. Define sexual harassment and explain its various forms.

I. MANAGERS AND THE HUMAN RESOURCE MANAGEMENT PROCESS
A. Introduction
  1. The quality of an organization is determined by
  2. Staffing and human resource management decisions and methods are
  3. Exhibit 6-1 introduces
  4. The first three steps represent
  5. Orientation and training and development
  6. The HRM process helps to
  7. The external environment

II. THE LEGAL ENVIRONMENT OF HRM
A. The Expanding Influence of the Federal Government
  1. See Exhibit 6-2 for examples.
  2. Equal employment opportunities
     a) Example — a community fire department
  3. Balancing the "shoulds and should-nots"
  4. Managers are not

III. EMPLOYMENT PLANNING
A. Defined
  1. Employment planning is
  2. Employment planning translates

B. How Does an Organization Conduct an Employee Assessment?
1. Management begins by
2. Another part of the current assessment is the job analysis.
3. Job analysis is
   a) The purpose of job analysis is
4. A job description is
5. It typically portrays
6. The job specification states
7. It identifies
8. Their importance for recruiting and selecting is in the fact that

C. How Are Future Employee Needs Determined?
1. Future human resource needs are determined by
2. Demand for human resources is a result of
3. The overall organizational goals and the resulting revenue forecast
4. After assessing current capabilities and future needs

IV. RECRUITMENT AND SELECTION
A. Where Does a Manager Look to Recruit Candidates?
1. Candidates can be found by using several sources—including the World Wide Web.
   a) See Exhibit 6-3.
2. The source that is used should reflect
3. Certain recruiting sources produce superior candidates.
4. How does a manager handle layoffs?
5. What are a manager's downsizing options?
6. Exhibit 6-4 summarizes

B. Is There a Basic Premise to Selecting Job Candidates?
1. The selection process is
2. "Successful" means
3. Any selection decision can
   a) Shown in Exhibit 6-5.
4. A decision is correct when
5. Problems occur, however, when
6. Reliability addresses
7. What is validity?

C. How Effective Are Tests and Interviews as Selection Devices?
1. Managers can reduce
2. The best-known devices include
3. How do written tests serve a useful purpose?
   a) Typical written tests
   b) Tests of intellectual ability,
   c) Intelligence tests
4. What are performance-simulation tests?
   a) They are based on
   b) Performance-simulation tests are
   c) The advantage
   d) They are also

D. Is the Interview Effective?
1. The interview,
2. The value of the interview is
3. Interviews are
4. The typical interview
5. List the kinds of potential biases
6. Managers can make interviews more valid and reliable.
7. How can you close the deal?
    a) Selling applicants
    b) Every job applicant acquires
    c) Excessively inflated information
8. An RJP

V. ORIENTATION, TRAINING, AND DEVELOPMENT
A. How Do We Introduce New Hires to the Organization?
1. Once selected, the job candidate needs to be
2. The major objectives of orientation
3. Job orientation
4. Work-unit orientation
5. Organization orientation informs
6. Management has an obligation

B. What Is Employee Training?
1. Employee training is
2. It involves changing
3. Determining training needs
    a) See Exhibit 6-6.
4. Warning signals
5. How are employees trained?
6. What are some of the typical methods used?
7. How can managers ensure that training is working?

VI. PERFORMANCE MANAGEMENT
A. What Is a Performance Management System?
1. A performance management system is
2. Specific techniques—see Exhibit 6-8.
3. The written essay
4. Critical incidents
5. Graphic rating scales
6. Behaviorally anchored rating scales (BARS).
7. The 360-degree appraisal.
8. Traditional performance evaluations systems may be
9. The 360-degree feedback process
10. Research studies into the effectiveness of 360-degree performance appraisals

B. Should We Compare People with One Another or against Some Set Standards?
1. Multi-person comparisons
2. The group order ranking
3. The individual ranking approach
4. In the paired comparison approach

C. Isn't MBO an Appraisal Approach, Too?
1. MBO is
2. Employees are evaluated by
3. MBO's popularity

D. What Happens When Performance Falls Short?
1. If an employee is not performing in a satisfactory manner
2. A manager needs to find out why.
    a)
    b)
    c)
3. Employee counseling is

VII. COMPENSATION AND BENEFITS
A. How Are Pay Levels Determined?
1. The goals of compensation administration are
2. The primary determination of pay is
3. Pay levels
4. The most important factor is

B. Why Do Organizations Offer Employee Benefits?
1. An organization has to take into account
2. The benefits offered by an organization
3. Most are required to provide

VIII. CURRENT ISSUES IN HUMAN RESOURCES MANAGEMENT
A. How Can Workforce Diversity Be Managed?
1. How does workforce diversity affect recruitment, selection, and orientation?
2. Improving workforce diversity requires
3. Once a diverse set of applicants exists
4. Orientation is

B. What Is Sexual Harassment?
1. Sexual harassment is
2. Sexual harassment is defined as
3. Much of the problem is
4. The EEOC cites three situations
5. For many organizations, it's
6. The Supreme Court case of *Meritor Savings Bank vs. Vinson*
7. What can a company do to protect itself?
8. The courts want to know two things
9. In June 1998, the Supreme Court ruled that sexual harassment
10. The case of *Jerold Mackenzie vs. Miller Brewing*
11. What the Mackenzie case tells us is

C. How Can Organizations Be Family-Friendly?
1. Family-friendly benefits are
2. At the heart of such programs is
3. Family-friendly benefits are also addressing
4. Examples of Johnson & Johnson and Stratco.

    5. Another family concern,

    6. An organization's human resource management policies need

D. Can Unions and Management Cooperate?
    1. Historically, the relationship between a labor union and management was built on conflict.

    2. But management

    3. Some labor unions have

    4. Current U.S. labor laws

    5. The National Labor Relations Act

    6. The current legal environment

E. Can Mangers Prevent Workplace Violence?
    1. A much greater emphasis today is

    2. This is not just a U.S. phenomenon.

    3. Two factors have contributed greatly to this

    4. How to prevent the violence from occurring on the job—and to reduce their liability.

       a)

       b)

       c)

F. How Do "Survivors" Respond to Layoffs?
    1. Many organizations have

    2. Some affected individuals

    3. Very little has been done for

    4. A new syndrome

    5. Managers may want to

    6. Group discussions can

REVIEW QUESTIONS
1. What are the key elements in the strategic human resource process? Can you diagram the process in terms of your college or a company you've worked for?
   Answer – Pages 185-186

2. Chart the key human resources laws and what protections they offer workers.
   Answer – Pages 186-187, Exhibit 6-2

3. Explain the role and function of a human resources inventory, a job analysis, a job description, and a job specification.
   Answer – Page 188

4. What is the relationship between selection, recruitment, and job analysis, job description, and job specification?
   Answer – Pages 188-192

5. Explain the various potential outcomes of the selection decision.
   Answer – Pages 191-192

6. What are the key considerations involved in the use of each potential selection device available to managers?
   Answer – Pages 192-195

7. What are the major problems of the interview as a selection device?
   Answer – Pages 193-195

8. What are the roles of orientation and employee training and how to the relate to one another?
   Answer – Pages 196-198

9. Create a table of the various performance appraisal methods with their advantages and disadvantages.
   Answer – Page 199

10. What is the relationship of performance appraisal and performance management?
    Answer – Page 199

11. How are compensation strategies and levels determined?
    Answer – Pages 202-203

12. Outline the various forms of sexual harassment. What are a manager's responsibilities once sexual harassment is reported to him/her?
    Answer – Pages 204-206

13. What can managers do about workplace violence?
    Answer – Pages 208-209

STUDY QUIZ
Multiple Choice Questions

1. Those steps of the strategic human resource process that help employees adapt to the organization and keep their skills current are:
   a) planning and performance appraisal.
   b) orientation and training.
   c) recruitment and compensation.
   d) safety and health and selection.

2. _____ tells management what individual employees can do.
   a) Job analysis
   b) Job specification
   c) Job description
   d) Human resource inventory

3. If a manager needs to immediately reduce her work force size temporarily due to a temporary downturn in business, she would use _____ as her downsizing option.
   a) firings
   b) attrition
   c) layoffs
   d) early retirements

4. The selection device that has moderate validity predictability for intellectual ability, spatial ability, motor skills, etc., for semi-skilled and unskilled jobs is:
   a) a written test.
   b) an interview.
   c) performance-simulation test.
   d) an assessment center.

5. A selection tool that provides job candidates with both positive and negative information about the job and the company so they can make an informed and reasonable decision regarding employment is known as:
   a) a performance-simulation test.
   b) an employee orientation.
   c) human resource assessment.
   d) a realistic job preview.

6. When doing a training needs assessment, once a manager reviews the organization's strategic goals, his/her next step is to:
   a) determine the skill or knowledge deficiencies of the individual employee related to those goals.
   b) decide what tasks need to be completed to accomplish those tasks.
   c) chose what behaviors are necessary for each jobholder to complete his/her job duties.
   d) decide which if any additional human resources are needed.

7. One of the oldest and most popular performance management tools that lists performance factors and permits evaluating on an incremental scale is/are known as:
   a) critical incidents
   b) MBO
   c) multiperson
   d) graphic rating scales

8. The performance feedback process that is growing in popularity that gives employees feedback from several sources, their bosses, peers, customers, etc., is known as:
   a) 360-degree appraisal.
   b) multiperson appraisal.
   c) graphic rating scales.
   d) critical incidents.

9. If a manager wanted to compare the employee performance of several employees he might choose to use the _____ performance appraisal tool
   a) MBO
   b) paired comparison approach
   c) 360-degree appraisal
   d) BARS

10. Compensation may be directly affected by a number of factors including:
    a) the company's industry.
    b) employee skills and abilities.
    c) geographic location.
    d) employee seniority.

11. The kinds of situations that constitute sexual harassment include:
    a) verbal or physical conduct that creates a hostile environment.
    b) verbal or physical conduct that unreasonably interferes with an individual's work.
    c) verbal or physical conduct that adversely affects an employee's employment opportunities.
    d) all of these.

12. Family-friendly benefits include:
    a) heath insurance.
    b) sick leave.
    c) on-site child care.
    d) all of these.

13. Which of the following constitutes a legal employee-involvement program?
    a) A project improvement team lead by a first line supervisor.
    b) A self-managed work team responsible for planning, conducting and monitoring its own work.
    c) A quality circle group that identifies problems, recommends solution, and receives approval fro implementation of suggestions by upper management.
    d) All of these.

14. Experts argue that there are two trends in the United States that contribute to workplace violence: disgruntled employees and:
    a) domestic violence.   208
    b) affirmative action programs.
    c) a downturn in the economy.
    d) improperly implemented diversity training programs.

15. A commonly neglected element in layoffs is:
    a) the laid-off workers themselves.
    b) laid-off managers.
    c) survivors of the layoff.
    d) government regulations relevant to the layoff.

True/False Questions

1. The human resource planning process consists of recruiting, orientation, and performance management.

2. The Civil Rights Act of 1964 prohibits pay differences on the basis of gender for equal work, prohibits age discrimination, among its other better known prohibitions.

3. The primary determinant of human resource needs is the company's strategic direction.

4. The best source for recruiting new employees is on-campus college recruiting.

5. A good hiring decision has been made when either an applicant predicted to be successful is hired and when a candidate who is predicted to be unsuccessful is not hired.

6. A selection device is valid when it clearly measures job-related criteria.

7. The most commonly used selection device is the performance-simulation test.

8. Interviews are most valid for determining applicant intelligence, motivation, and interpersonal skills.

9. Basic to determining training needs are the organization's strategic goals.

10. Critical incidents performance measurement tool is a behavioral-based, highly quantified, relatively quick and easy-to-use tool.

11. While an excellent goal-setting tool, MBO can also be used as a performance management device.

12. Generally speaking, employee orientation is more difficult for women and minorities.

13. A woman cannot sexually harass a man nor can individuals of the same gender sexually harass each other.

14. United States labor law assumes an adversarial relationship between unions and management.

15. Central to legal employee involvement programs is that the employees have the power to make decisions and act independently of management.

Answers to Chapter 6 Study Quiz

Multiple Choice (Page - Answer)

1. b-186	6. b-197	11. d-205
2. d-188	7. d-199	12. c-206
3. c-191	8. a-200	13. b-207
4. a-193	9. b-201	14. a-208
5. d-195	10. b-202	15. c-209

True/False

1. F-185	6. T-192	11. T-201
2. F-187	7. F-193	12. T-204
3. F-189	8. T-195	13. F-205
4 F-189	9. T-197	14. T-204
5. T-191	10. F-199	15. T-207

CAREER MODULE
INTRODUCTION

Use the Outline to Guide Your Note Taking from the Text

Considerations as you read

As you read and take notes, think about these questions: they will help you organize your study notes.
1. Outline the three-step career self-assessment process.
2. What are some good job hunting sources on the Internet?
3. Can you explain how to create the best impression in a job interview?
4. Review the tactics for successful career management.
5. What are the factors that contribute to the development of stress in workers' lives?
6. Define or describe innovation and creativity in an organizational context, and discuss ways each can be encouraged.

I. INTRODUCTION
A. A Career
1. It can mean
2. A career as the sequence of
3. Always an important topic, there have been some drastic changes in recent years.
   a)
   b)
4. Today, the individual

II. MAKING A CAREER DECISION
A. Introduction
1. The best choice offers
2. A good career match is one

B. Career Planning—A Three-Step, Self-Assessment Process
1. Identify and
2. Convert this information into
3. Test your career possibilities against

III. GETTING INTO THE ORGANIZATION
A. Introduction
1. One of the more stressful situations you will face
2. Tips that may increase your chances of finding employment.
   a)
   b)
   c)

B. Where Can I Find Jobs Advertised on the Internet?
1. There has been a proliferation of Web sites that provide job searchers with information.
2. See your text for the list of the more popular sites.

C. How Do I Prepare My Resume?

1. Your resume is typically
   a) It must
   b) It must
   c) See Exhibit CM-1.
2. Key themes regarding resumes.
   a) The resume must be
   b) The style
   c) Companies use
   d) Use good quality
3. An electronic resume
   a) Many of the same principles hold true.
   b) You'll need to be able to
4. Proofread
   a) The resume is the only
5. The cover letter
   a) It tells the recruiter
   b) Describe
   c) Offer reasons
   d) Cover letters should be
   e) Address it to
6. If everything else fails,
7. Like the resume, the cover letter should be
8. Sign each cover letter individually.

D. Are There Ways to Excel at the Interview?

1. Interviews
2. Interviews are so popular because
3. It's important for you to understand
4. Many of the biases
5. Impression management refers to
6. Research has shown that
7. How can you increase your chances of
   a)
   b)
   c)
   d)
   e)
   f)
   g)
   h)
   i)
   j)
   k)

E. What Are Some Suggestions for Developing a Successful Management Career?

1. Keys to success— see Exhibit CM-2.
2. Select your first job
3. Participate in an
4. Do
5. Present

6. Learn the
7. Gain control of
8. Stay visible.
9. Don't stay
10. Find a
11. Support
12. Stay
13. Think
14. Keep your skills
15. Develop

REVIEW QUESTIONS

1. What are the three steps of the self-assessment process? Explain each.
   Answer – Page 218

2. What are the important considerations in preparing the best job resume?
   Answer – Pages 219-221

3. What is impression management, and how can it help you excel in a job interview?
   Answer – Pages 221-223

4. Outline the various tactics offered for managing your career.
   Answer – Pages 223-227

STUDY QUIZ
Multiple Choice Questions

1. When selecting a career, a key concern is the fit between:
   a) your salary and your lifestyle.
   b) what you want from life and what you need.
   c) your commitment and your industry.
   d) the current hot industry and your career.

2. When conducting a self-assessment, you should begin with:
   a) identifying and organizing your skills, interests, needs, and values.
   b) a study of the general career fields available to you.
   c) testing your career possibilities through an internship or shadowing program.
   d) choosing a career field.

3. The primary information source used by a recruiter in determining whether to grant you an interview is:
   a) your cover letter.
   b) your academic transcript.
   c) your resume.
   d) their application form.

4. A good cover letter:
   a) is printed on quality paper.
   b) is addressed to an actual person.
   c) explains why the resume was sent.
   d) does all of these.

5. Studies suggest that the interviewer draws 80% perception of you from:
   a) your cover letter.
   b) your resume.
   c) your interview.
   d) his/her initial impression.

6. When developing your career, it is important that you:
   a) take the best paying job initially, as it sets your career pay scale.
   b) participate in an internship program as a student.
   c) avoid the power structure and politics of your company.
   d) stay at least 3-5 years on your first job.

True/False Questions

1. Employees have always been responsible for their own careers.

2. It is best for college students to begin their job search in the fall of their senior year.

3. It is important when writing your resume that you use unique language and expressions to make it as distinct as possible from other resumes.

4. Cover letter should always be addressed to an individual, not "To whom it may concern."

5. Preparation for the interview is almost as important as your conduct during the interview when it comes to impression management.

6. You should avoid practicing interviewing so that you will be fresh and unrehearsed in your actual job interviews.

7. When developing your career, your first job is relatively unimportant because it is only a stepping stone and doesn't require a great deal of thought in its selection.

8. Image is very important in the management and maintenance of your career.

9. Generally, it makes good career sense to support your boss even when you don't fully agree with his/her decisions.

Answers to Chapter 6a - Career Module Study Quiz

Multiple Choice (Page - Answer)

1. b-217
2. a-218
3. c-219

4. d-221
5. d-222
6. b-223

True/False

1. F-217
2. T-219
3. F-220
4. T-221
5. T-222

6. F-223
7. F-223
8. T-225
9. T-226

CHAPTER 7 - MANAGING CHANGE AND INNOVATION

LEARNING OUTCOMES
After reading this chapter, you should be able to:
1. Describe what change variables are within a manager's control.
2. Identify external and internal forces for change.
3. Explain how managers can serve as change agents.
4. Contrast the "calm waters" and "white water rapids" metaphors for change. Explain why people are likely to resist change.
5. Describe techniques for reducing resistance to change.
6. Identify what is meant by the term *organization development*, and specify four popular OD techniques.
7. Explain the causes and symptoms of stress.
8. Differentiate between creativity and innovation.
9. Explain how organizations can stimulate innovation.

Use the Outline to Guide Your Note Taking from the Text

Considerations as you read

As you read and take notes, think about these questions; they will help you organize your study notes.
1. Outline the external and internal forces that create the need for change.
2. In what circumstances are the "calm waters" and "white water" metaphors of change valid?
3. Why do people resist change, and how can these reasons be overcome?
4. Create a table of the various OD techniques and what each does for the manager as a change agent.
5. What are the factors that contribute to the development of stress in workers' lives?
6. Define or describe innovation and creativity in an organizational contex, and discuss ways each can be encouraged.

I. WHAT IS CHANGE?
A. Introduction
1. Change is
2. If it weren't for change
    a) Planning
    b) Organization design
    c) Decision making
3. Change is an
4. Handling change is
5. A manager can change three things.
    a)
    b)
    c)
    d) See Exhibit 7-1.

B. Forces for Change
1. There are both
2. These same forces

C. What Are the External Forces Creating a Need for Change?
  1. They come from various sources.

     a)
     b)
     c)
     d)

D. What Are the Internal Forces Creating a Need for Change?
  1. Internal forces tend to
  2. When management redefines

E. How Can a Manager Serve as a Change Agent?
  1. Changes within an organization need a catalyst.
  2. People who act as catalysts
     a) Any manager can
     b) A nonmanager can
  3. For major systemwide changes
     a) Outside consultants
     b) But they may
     c) They are also
  4. Internal managers who act as change agents may be:
     a)
     b)

F. Two Views on the Change Process
  1. The "calm waters" metaphor
     a) Change surfaces as
  2. The "white water rapids" metaphor
     a) Change is a

G. What Is the "Calm Waters" Metaphor?
  1. The "calm waters" metaphor
     a) The prevailing model for handling change in calm waters is
     b) See Exhibit 7-2.
  2. According to Lewin
     a) The status quo can be
  3. Unfreezing is
     a)
     b)
     c)
  4. Once unfreezing
  5. The new situation needs to be
     a) Unless this is done
     b) The objective of refreezing is to
  6. Lewin's three-step process

H. What Is the "White Water Rapids" Metaphor?
  1. The "white water" metaphor
     a) Variable college curriculum example.
  2. The stability and predictability

      3. Many of today's managers face

      4. Is the white water rapids metaphor merely an overstatement?

I. Does Every Manager Face a World of Constant and Chaotic Change?

      1. Not every manager faces

      2. Few organizations today can

          a) Most competitive advantages

          b) People's Express was described as the model

          c) Southwest Airlines, and USAirways Metrojet

      3. Tom Peters,

II. ORGANIZATIONAL CHANGE AND MEMBER RESISTANCE

A. Introduction

      1. As change agents, managers

      2. Change can be

      3. It can be a threat to

B. Why Do People Resist Change?

      1. An individual is likely to resist change for three reasons

          a) See Exhibit 7-3.

      2. Changes substitute

          a) Employees in organizations

      3. The second cause of resistance is

          a)

          b)

          c)

      4. A final cause of resistance is

          a) If expressed positively, this form of resistance

C. What Are Some Techniques for Reducing Resistance to Organizational Change?

      1. Dysfunctional resistance

          a) See Exhibit 7-4.

      2. Education and communication

      3. Participation

      4. Facilitation and support

      5. Negotiation

      6. Manipulation and cooptation

      7. Coercion

III. MAKING CHANGES IN THE ORGANIZATION

A. What Can a Manager Change?

      1. Changing structure includes

      2. Changing technology encompasses

          a) The primary focus on technological change

          b) Employees

          c) Work processes must be

          d) This adaptability requires

      3. Changes in people refers to

          a) They require a workforce

          b) Again, necessitating

          c) It also demands

B. How Do Organizations Implement "Planned" Changes?
1. Most change in an organization
2. The effort to assist organizational members with a planned change is

C. What Is Organization Development?
1. Organization development (OD) is
2. Its focus is to
3. Organization leaders are
4. Fundamental to organization development is

D. Are There Typical OD Techniques?
1. Any organizational activity that assists with implementing planned change
2. The more popular OD efforts
3. Survey feedback
   a) Employees are
   b) The data the change agent obtains
4. In process consultation
   a) These might include
   b) Consultants are not there to
5. Team building is
   a) The primary focus is
6. Intergroup development attempts to

IV. STRESS: THE AFTERMATH OF ORGANIZATIONAL CHANGE

A. What Is Stress?
1. Stress is
2. It is a complex issue.
3. Stress can manifest itself in
   a)
   b)
4. Constraints are
   a) They inhibit
5. Demands
6. When coupled with uncertainty
7. When constraints or demands have an effect
8. It is important to recognize that
   a) A Northwestern National Life Insurance study
9. And stress on the job
   a) In Japan, there is a concept called karoshi
10. Employees in Germany and Britain

B. Are There Common Causes of Stress?
1. Factors that create stress
   a) See Exhibit 7-6.
2. Task demands are
   a)
   b)
   c)

94

3. Role demands relate to
   a) Role conflicts
   b) Role overload
   c) Role ambiguity
4. Interpersonal demands are
5. Organization structure can
   a) Excessive rules and
6. Organizational leadership represents
7. Personal factors that can create stress include
   a)
   b)
   c) Type A behavior is
   d) Type B's

C. What Are the Symptoms of Stress?
1. There are three general ways that stress reveals itself.
2. Most of the early interest over stress focused
   a) High stress levels result in
   b) Detecting these requires
3. Of greater importance to managers are
4. The psychological symptoms
5. The behaviorally related symptoms

D. How Can Stress Be Reduced?
1. Some stress in organizations is
2. Make sure that employees are
3. Letting employees know
4. Redesigning jobs
5. Regardless
6. Employee assistance programs
7. Since their early focus on
   a) One of the most notable is the use of EAPs to help control
8. A wellness program is
   a) These programs may include
   b) Wellness programs are designed to

V. STIMULATING INNOVATION
A. "Innovate or die!"
1. The rallying cry of today's managers.
2. The standard of innovation
3. Management at 3M
4. What's the secret to 3M's success?

B. How Are Creativity and Innovation Related?
1. Creativity means
2. An organization that stimulates creativity
3. Innovation is the process of
   a) Custom Foot, a Connecticut-based shoe manufacturer,
   b) Another example Novo Nordisk,
4. The innovative organization is characterized by

5. The 3M Company is aptly described as
6. So, too, is the highly successful microchip manufacturer Intel.

C. What Is Involved in Innovation?
1. Some people believe that
2. Creativity can be viewed as
3. Perception
4. Ideas go though a process of
   a) During this
5. Inspiration in the creative process is
6. Creative work requires
   a) Innovation involves
   b) Thomas Edison is often
   c) That 99 percent, or the innovation, involves

D. How Can a Manager Foster Innovation?
1. There are three sets of variables that have been found to stimulate innovation:

E. How Do Structural Variables Affect Innovation?
1. First,
   a) They are lower in
2. Second, easy availability of
   a) An abundance of
3. Frequent inter-unit communication
   a) 3M, for instance, is

F. How Does an Organization's Culture Affect Innovation?
1. Innovative organizations tend to have similar cultures.
2. They encourage
3. They reward
   a) They celebrate
4. An innovative culture is likely to have the following seven characteristics:
   a)
   b)
   c)
   d)
   e)
   f)
   g)

G. What Human Resource Variables Affect Innovation?
1. Innovative organizations actively
2. Once a new idea is developed, champions of change
3. Research finds that champions have
4. Champions also display characteristics associated with
   a)
   b)
   c)

REVIEW QUESTIONS

1. What are the three things that managers can really change in an organization?
   Answer – Pages 231-232

2. Compare and contrast the "calm waters" and "white waters" metaphors for organizational change.
   Answer – Pages 232-234

3. Why do people resist change? Can you give an example of each type of resistance?
   Answer – Pages 235-237

4. How can managers reduce individual resistance?
   Answer – Page 237

5. What tools are available to managers in the implementation of planned change?
   Answer – Pages 238-239

6. What role do constraints and demands play in the creation of stress?
   Answer – Pages 240-241

7. What are EAP and wellness programs, and how can they help employees manage stress?
   Answer – Pages 243-245

8. Outline the ways a manager can foster innovation in his/her organization.
   Answer – Pages 247-248

STUDY QUIZ
Multiple Choice Questions

1. There are a number of external forces that create a need for change in an organization; such as:
   a) technology.
   b) its workforce.
   c) its product line.
   d) all of these.

2. When a manager operates as a change agent:
   a) he/she tends to offer an objective perspective on the change.
   b) he/she will offer fairly drastic changes.
   c) he/she will have a good understanding of the firm's history, culture, etc.
   d) all of these things tend to happen.

3. Lewin's model of change:
   a) works best in the dynamic environment of the "white water" metaphor.
   b) disturbs an organization's equilibrium and requires refreezing in order to be maintained.
   c) can best be described by the motto, "if it ain't broke, fix it anyway."
   d) includes all of these.

4.   In the view of the "water water" metaphor, research seems to show that most company's competitive advantage only lasts about:
  a)   6 months.
  b)   9 months.
  c)   18 months.
  d)   3 years.

5.   Tom is a division VP. A company reorganization will save his company millions over the next few years, he will keep his VP job but manage a totally different business unit, yet Tom is strongly opposed to the change. What is the most likely reason for Tom's resistance?
  a)   fear of the unknown
  b)   fear of losing something of value
  c)   belief the change is not good for the organization
  d)   concern for the laid off employees

6.   Your college is restructuring its maintenance functions. The employees do not understand why the change is being made and wild rumors about contract service replacing them etc., have naturally aroused strong opposition. The best reduction of resistance strategy would be:
  a)   facilitation and negotiation.
  b)   coercion.
  c)   manipulation and cooptation.
  d)   education and communication.

7.   Your company is introducing a change effort to address poor employee attitudes, poor morale, and to increase employee productivity. This effort is most likely focusing on changing:
  a)   technology.
  b)   structure.
  c)   people.
  d)   none of these.

8.   An OD change effort where outside consultants are used to evaluate workflows, informal workunit relationships, formal communication channels, etc., and either offer solutions or help managers find experts who can help is:
  a)   survey feedback.
  b)   intergroup development.
  c)   team building.
  d)   process consulting.

9.   _____ is the force an employee feels when facing opportunities, demands, or constraints on him/her in his/her work setting.
  a)   *Karoshi*
  b)   Cognitive dissonance
  c)   Stress
  d)   Resistance to change

10. Jim is feeling a lot of stress due to his working conditions, the lack of control he has over his job, and his dependency on others—who are less productive—for input to his process. The origins of Jim's stress are most likely to be:
  a)   role demands.
  b)   task demands.
  c)   organizational structure.
  d)   interpersonal demands.

11. A type B personality:
    a) is characterized by a constant sense of urgency.
    b) has difficulty enjoying leisure time.
    c) leads to a much longer lifespan than Type A.
    d) is as susceptible to stress as a Type A.

12. The original focus of employee assistance programs was:
    a) family violence.
    b) alcohol abuse.
    c) relocation and adjustment of families.
    d) employee orientation to the company.

13. The innovation process generally begins with:
    a) goal setting.
    b) inspiration.
    c) incubation of an idea.
    d) perception.

14. An innovative organization is often characterized by:
    a) low levels of conflict.
    b) a strong emphasis on the practical.
    c) acceptance of ambiguity.
    d) all of these and more.

15. Those human resources variables that seem to have the clearest effect on innovation are:
    a) training and development.
    b) employee orientation.
    c) strong base salary and benefits program.
    d) all of these.

True/False Questions

1. Change is basically an alteration in an organization's environment, structure, technology, or people.

2. Internal forces for change may originate from either internal forces or be due to reaction to the impact of external change.

3. If you want to prepare a firm for change, according to Kurt Lewin's change model, you can simply increase the restraining forces that support the existing equilibrium.

4. The white-water metaphor sees the company's environment as both dynamic and uncertain.

5. Employees may resist change because of a fear of loss, a fear of uncertainty, or because they think the change is bad for the organization.

6. The basic difference between manipulation and cooptation and coercion is that the former is covert and subtle, the latter direct and overt.

7. The best OD technique for evaluating employee attitude about their perceptions regarding a change is team building.

8. Stress can be positive or negative depending on the individual's reaction to it.

9. A significant source of stress is interpersonal demands, when the role a person plays, or his/her workload creates conflicts and is too much for him/her to get done.

10. Early research on stress focused on the psychological symptoms.

11. EAPs now have a significant role in reducing a company's health insurance costs.

12. Creativity is the ability to combine ideas in a unique way or make unusual connections.

13. Key to innovation is the ability to turn inspiration into a useful product or service.

14. A mechanistic structure provides the necessary security to employees permitting them to give maximum attention to innovation.

15. A focus on ends rather than means and providing an open systems focus both characterize innovative organizations.

Answers to Chapter 7 Study Quiz

Multiple Choice (Page - Answer)

1. a-231	6. d-237	11. d-243
2. c-232	7. c-238	12. b-244
3. b-233	8. d-239	13. d-246
4. c-355	9. c-240	14. c-247
5. a-235	10. b-241	15. a-248

True/False

1. T-230	6. T-238	11. T-244
2. T-232	7. F-239	12. T-245
3. F-233	8. T-240	13. T-247
4. T-234	9. F-242	14. F-247
5. T-236	10. F-243	15. T-248

PART 4 - LEADING
CHAPTER 8 - FOUNDATIONS OF INDIVIDUAL AND GROUP BEHAVIOR

LEARNING OUTCOMES
After reading this chapter, you should be able to:
1. Define the focus and goals of organizational behavior.
2. Identify and describe the three components of attitudes.
3. Explain cognitive dissonance.
4. Describe the Myers-Briggs personality type framework and its use in organizations.
5. Define perception and describe the factors that can shape or distort perception.
6. Explain how managers can shape employee behavior.
7. Contrast formal and informal groups.
8. Explain why people join groups.
9. State how roles and norms influence employees' behavior.
10. Describe how group size affects group behavior.

Use the Outline to Guide Your Note Taking from the Text

Considerations as you read

As you read and take note, think about these questions: they will help you organize your study notes.
1. What part do attitudes play in the study of organizational behavior?
2. What is cognitive dissonance, and how is understanding it helpful in managing organizational behavior?
3. Can you compare and contrast the Myers-Briggs and the Big Five personality models?
4. What personality traits actually matter in predicting work behavior?
5. How might you use personality to better match individuals to jobs?
6. Define attribution theory and discuss how it can affect managers' perceptions.
7. Outline the shortcuts managers and nonmanagers use to judge others.
8. Discuss how operant conditioning, social learning theory, and shaping are used by managers to manage employee behavior.
9. Review the basic concepts or elements of a group. What makes a group a group?

I. TOWARD EXPLAINING AND PREDICTING BEHAVIOR
A. Organizational Behavior
   1. OB is
   2. It addresses
      a) See Exhibit 8-1.

B. What Is the Focus of Organizational Behavior?
   1. First, OB looks
      a) Psychologists
      b) Including
   2. Second, OB is concerned with
      a) Sociologists
      b) Which includes

C. What Are the Goals of Organizational Behavior?
   1. To explain and to
   2. The manager needs to understand
   3. The emphasis will be on

D. The Goals of OB Are to Explain and Predict Behavior
1. Attitudes are
2. An attitude is
3. The cognitive component
4. The affective component
5. The behavioral component
6. The three most important job-related attitudes are
    a) Job satisfaction is
    b) Job involvement is
    c) Organizational commitment represents

E. Do an Individual's Attitude and Behavior Need to Be Consistent?
1. People change
2. People seek
3. Individuals try to

F. What Is Cognitive Dissonance Theory?
1. Leon Festinger,
2. This theory
    a) Dissonance
    b) Cognitive dissonance refers to
3. Any form of inconsistency is
4. Festinger proposed
5. When the factors creating the dissonance are
6. The degree of influence that individuals believe
7. If they perceive the dissonance to be
8. The dissonance-producing behaviors
9. These moderating factors suggest that

G. How Can an Understanding of Attitudes Help Managers Be More Effective?
1. There is relatively strong evidence that
2. Managers should
    a) The pressure to reduce the dissonance is
    b) The pressure is also lessened if
3. Past research studies suggested that satisfied employees
4. But their effect on productivity was questioned.
5. Research in the early 1990s

II. PERSONALITY
A. Can Personality Predict Behavior?
1. Many of these personality characteristics are used to describe an individual's behavior.
2. The more popular of these traits include
3. Researchers attempted to focus on
4. Two widely recognized efforts.
    a) The Myers-Briggs Type Indicator.
    b) The five-factor model of personality.

B. What Is the Myers-Briggs Type Indicator?
1. One of the more
2. It uses four dimensions
   a) See Exhibit 8-2.
3. The sixteen personality types are
4. Extroversion versus introversion (EI).
   a)
   b)
5. Sensing versus intuitive (SN).
   a)
   b)
6. Thinking versus feeling (TF).
   a)
   b)
7. Judging versus perceiving (JP).
   a)
   b)
8. Proponents of the instrument believe

C. What Is the Big-Five Model of Personality?
1. The MBTI suffers from one major criticism
2. The Big-Five model
3. The Big Five factors are:
   a) Extroversion
   b) Agreeableness
   c) Conscientiousness
   d) Emotional stability
   e) Openness to experience
4. Research has shown
   a) One study reviewed five categories of occupations: professionals.
   b) Job performance was
   c) The results of the study showed
   d) Predictions
      (1) Extroversion
      (2) Openness to experience
      (3) Emotional security

D. What Is Emotional Intelligence?
1. Emotional intelligence (EI) refers to
2. It's composed of five dimensions.
   a) Self-awareness
   b) Self-management
   c) Self-motivation
   d) Empathy
   e) Social skills
3. Several studies suggest EI
   a) Bell Lab engineers
   b) A second study of Air Force recruiters
4. Forty percent of human resource managers felt that

E. Can Personality Traits Predict Practical Work-Related Behaviors?
1. Five personality traits are
2. Locus of control.
    a)
    b)
    c)
3. Machiavellianism
    a)
    b)
    c)
    d)
4. Self-esteem
    a)
    b)
    c)
    d)
5. Self-monitoring
    a)
    b)
    c)
    d)
6. Risk propensity
    a)
    b)
    c)
    d)

F. How Do We Match Personalities and Jobs?
1. Efforts have been made to match the proper personalities with the proper jobs.
2. The best-documented personality-job fit theory
3. Holland identified six basic personality types.
    a) See exhibit 8-3.
    b) Holland's research supports the hexagonal diagram in Exhibit 8-4.
    c) The closer two fields
4. The theory argues that
5. The key points of the model.
    a) There do appear to be
    b) There are
    c) People in job environments congruent
    d) Satisfied and

G. How Can an Understanding of Personality Help Managers Be More Effective?
1. The major value probably lies in selection.
2. More higher performing
3. Also a manager can better understand

H. Do Personality Attributes Differ across National Cultures?
   1. There certainly are no
   2. Yet a country's culture should
   3. Example locus of control.
      a) North Americans
      b) Middle Eastern countries

III. PERCEPTION

A. Defined
   1. Perception is
   2. Research demonstrates that

B. What Influences Perception?
   1. A number of factors operate to
   2. They reside
   3. The individual's personal characteristics will
   4. The characteristics of the target
   5. Targets are not
      a) See Exhibit 8-5.
   6. The context in which we see objects

C. How Do Managers Judge Employees?
   1. Much of the research on perception is
   2. Our perceptions of people differ
   3. When we observe people
   4. These assumptions have led researchers to

D. What Is Attribution Theory?
   1. It was proposed to explain
   2. The theory suggests that
      a) Internally caused
      b) Externally caused
   3. That determination depends on three factors
   4. Distinctiveness
   5. Consensus
   6. Consistency
   7. Exhibit 8-6 summarizes the key elements in attribution theory.

E. Can Attributions Be Distorted?
   1. There are errors or biases that distort attributions.
   2. We have a tendency to
      a) This is called
   3. There is also a tendency for individuals to
      a) This is called

F. What Shortcuts Do Managers Use in Judging Others?
   1. Managers use a number of shortcuts to judge others.
   2. Individuals develop techniques
   3. These techniques can and do get us into trouble.
      a) To understand the distortions see Exhibit 8-7.
   4. Individuals

    5. Assumed similarity
    6. Stereotyping.
    7. The halo effect
    8. Self-fulfilling prophecy

G. How Can an Understanding of Perceptions Help Managers Be More Effective?
    1. Managers need to recognize that
    2. Managers should pay close attention to

IV. LEARNING
A. Defined
    1. A psychologist's definition
    2. A workable definition of learning is
    3. Two popular theories

B. What Is Operant Conditioning?
    1. Behavior is
    2. People behave
        a) Reinforcement
    3. Building on earlier work
        a) Behavior is
        b) Creating pleasing consequences
        c) Rewards
        d) Behavior
    4. Operant learning
    5. If a behavior fails to be positively reinforced

C. What Is Social Learning Theory?
    1. Learning through
    2. It is an extension of
    3. People respond to
    4. The influence of models is
    5. Four processes determine the influence that a model will have on an individual.
        a) Attentional
        b) Retention
        c) Motor reproduction
        d) Reinforcement

D. How Can Managers Shape Behavior?
    1. Managers often attempt to
    2. We shape behavior by
    3. There are four ways in which to shape behavior.
        a) Positive reinforcement
        b) Negative reinforcement.
        c) Punishment
        d) Extinction
    4. Both positive and negative reinforcement result
    5. Both punishment and extinction also result in

E. How Can an Understanding of Learning Help Managers Be More Effective?
1. Employees continually learn on the job.
2. Managers need to decide

V. FOUNDATIONS OF GROUP BEHAVIOR
A. What Is a Group?
1. A group is defined as
2. Groups can be either formal or informal.
   a) Formal groups are
   b) Informal groups are

B. Why Do People Join Groups?
1. There is no single reason why individuals join groups.
2. Most people join a group for the reasons listed in Exhibit 8-8.
3. Security
4. Status
5. Self-esteem
6. Affiliation
7. Power
8. Goal achievement

VI. What Are the Basic Concepts for Understanding Group Behaviors?
A. What Are Roles?
1. The concept of roles applies to
2. A role refers to
3. Individuals play
4. Employees attempt to
5. An individual who is
6. Employees in organizations often

B. How Do Norms and Conformity Affect Group Behavior?
1. All groups have
2. Norms
3. Common classes of norms
4. Work groups typically
5. These norms
6. Loyalty norms are
7. Individuals are susceptible to
8. The impact that group pressures for conformity

C. What Is Status, and Why Is It Important?
1. Status is
2. Status hierarchies
3. Status may be
4. Members of groups
5. It is important for employees to believe

D. Does Group Size Affect Group Behavior?
1. The effect on the group's behavior depends on what criteria you are looking at.
2. Small groups are
3. If engaged in problem solving

4. Large groups
5. Groups of approximately
6. As groups get incrementally larger
7. The total productivity of a group of four
8. The best explanation is
9. When the results of the group cannot be attributed to
10. When managers use work teams

E. Are Cohesive Groups More Effective?
1. The more the members are attracted to
2. Research has generally shown that
3. A key moderating variable is
   a) The more cohesive a group
   b) If these goals are favorable
   c) But if cohesiveness is high
   d) If cohesiveness is low
   e) When cohesiveness is low
4. See Exhibit 8-10.

REVIEW QUESTIONS
1. What is organizational behavior, its focus, and its goals?
   Answer – Pages 256-258

2. Identify the three components of an attitude and their importance for managers in managing organizational behavior.
   Answer – Pages 258-259

3. What is cognitive dissonance, and how do individuals manage it in their work lives?
   Answer – Pages 260-261

4. What does the Big Five model offer managers in understanding employee behavior that the Myers-Briggs does not?
   Answer – Pages 262-264

5. Explain emotional intelligence and its importance in organizations.
   Answer – Page 264

6. Which personality traits are important to managers for predicting work-related behaviors?
   Answer – Pages 264-266

7. How does perception affect manager's judgments about employees? What role does attribution theory play in managers' judgments?
   Answer – Pages 269-271

8. What shortcuts do managers use in making judgments about employees?
   Answer – Pages 271-273

9. Explain social learning theory and how managers can use it to help direct their employees.
   Answer – Pages 274-275

10. Why do people join groups?
    Answer – Pages 276-277

11. List and explain the basic concepts of group behavior.
    Answer – Pages 277-281

STUDY QUIZ
Multiple Choice Questions

1. A great deal of organizational behavior is hidden below the surface of the organization, such as:
   a) formal authority.
   b) strategies.
   c) group norms.
   d) chains of command.

2. Ben has a rather negative attitude about upper management and whenever he sees a member of upper management, he turns away so that he doesn't have to talk with him/her. This is an example of the ___ component of attitude.
   a) cognitive
   b) affective
   c) organizational
   d) behavioral

3. If a manager feels that the factors that are creating cognitive dissonance for him and that he has little influence or likelihood of influencing the situation, the pressure to deal with the dissonance will be:
   a) high.
   b) low.
   c) nonexistent.
   d) moderate.

4. The personality model/concept that addresses how someone thinks, processes information, perceives the world, and reflects that person's attitudes toward the external world is:
   a) the Big Five model.
   b) Emotional Intelligence.
   c) cognitive dissonance resolution.
   d) the Myers-Briggs type indicator.

5. The ability to persist in the face of setbacks and failures is a measure of one's ____ in terms of his/her emotional intelligence.
   a) self-motivation
   b) self-awareness
   c) social skills
   d) self-management

6. The measure of one's ability to adapt his/her behavior to accommodate external factors is the personality trait of:
   a) propensity for risk taking.
   b) social skills.
   c) self-monitoring.
   d) empathy.

7. An individual with a strong realistic orientation in Holland's typology, would do best in a job that was:
   a) social or realistic or enterprising.
   b) realistic or convention or investigative.
   c) artistic or investigative or social.
   d) realistic or enterprising or social.

8. One's perception is influenced by a number of factors, including:
   a) what one is are looking at.
   b) one's own experience.
   c) the circumstances surrounding the perception.
   d) all of these.

9. _____ is simply an explanation for how we make judgments about behavior and the reasons behind it.
   a) Perception
   b) Attribution theory
   c) Personality
   d) Operant conditioning

10. If a manager forms an impression of a job candidate or an employee based on a single demonstrated trait, the manager is using the perceptual shortcut of:
    a) selectivity.
    b) assumed similarity.
    c) stereotyping.
    d) halo effect.

11. Dennis is trying to train his salespeople to do their paperwork accurately and submit it on time. Each time they submit a report on time without errors, they earn points towards a night out on the town with their spouse. Dennis' reward system is an example of:
    a) cognition.
    b) social learning.
    c) operant conditioning.
    d) attentional learning.

12. _____ argues that people learn only when they recognize and pay attention to the critical elements of learning, when they remember the model's action, when they have the opportunity to practice what they've learned, etc.
    a) Social learning
    b) Shaping behavior
    c) Affective cognition
    d) Operant conditioning

13. If Tami gives verbal praise to her employees every time they provide exceptional customer service she is using positive reinforcement as part of:
    a) social learning.
    b) shaping behavior.
    c) attentional learning.
    d) affiliation affirmation.

14. When someone in a group informally keeps time for the group so they don't meet too long, and another person periodically summarizes the group's ideas, these two people are:
    a) shaping group norms.
    b) acting out their group roles.
    c) seeking status in the group.
    d) experiencing social loafing.

15. If a group is bothered by one of its members continually showing up late, this is an example of the group concept:
    a) norms.
    b) roles.
    c) cohesiveness.
    d) social loafing.

True/False Questions

1. Attitudes is a personality trait that measures the degree people feel they are in control of their own lives.

2. When someone experiences cognitive dissonance, he/she usually seeks to reduce or relieve that tension.

3. Current research shows that organizations were more successful with satisfied workers than those with less satisfied workers, but this does not mean a happy worker is a productive worker.

4. Research shows that consciousness in the Big Five model of personality is the most consistent indicator of job performance for all occupational groups tested.

5. High Mach employees are almost always "trouble" in that they can't be trusted.

6. Decision making accuracy was the same for both high-risk taking and low-risk taking managers according to one study.

7. If an employee can't find a job or career similar to their orientation on Holland's typology, their next best choice is a job or career in the opposite orientation on the hexagon.

8. There does seem to be some significant evidence for their being national "personality types," i.e., that a national culture tends to be dominated by one type of personality.

9. If someone behaves as we would expect others to behave in a given situation, then we would say that the individual's behavior demonstrates consensus.

10. The error employees make in distorting feedback, either positively or negatively is known as the self-serving bias.

11. Key to learning is the permanence of the change in behavior brought about by the learning.

12. In social learning theory the influence of the model is depending on several factors including whether or not the learning is reinforced.

13. Negative reinforcement and punishment are synonyms and both lead to the extinction of behavior.

14. People join groups for a number of reasons including the enhancing of their sense of self-worth.

15. Status in a group is earned from or conferred by the group on an individual.

Answers to Chapter 8 Study Quiz

Multiple Choice (Page - Answer)

1. c-257	6. c-266	11. c-273
2. d-258	7. b-267	12. a-274
3. b-260	8. d-269	13. b-275
4. d-262	9. b-270	14. b-277
5. a-264	10. d-272	15. a-278

True/False

1. F-257	6. T-266	11. T-273
2. F-260	7. F-268	12. T-275
3. T-261	8. F-268	13. F-275
4. T-264	9. T-270	14. T-276
5. F-265	10. T-271	15. T-279

CHAPTER 9 - UNDERSTANDING WORK TEAMS

LEARNING OUTCOMES
After reading this chapter, you should be able to:
1. Explain the growing popularity of work teams in organizations.
2. Describe the five stages of team development.
3. Contrast work groups with work teams.
4. Identify four common types of work teams.
5. List the characteristics of high-performing work teams.
6. Discuss how organizations can create team players.
7. Explain how managers can keep teams from becoming stagnant.
8. Describe the role of teams in continuous process improvement programs.

Use the Outline to Guide Your Note Taking from the Text

Considerations as you read

As you read and take notes, think about these questions: they will help you organize your study notes.
1. What characterizes each of the stages that a group moves through?
2. Compare and contrast work groups and work teams.
3. List and describe each of the various uses of teams in organizations.
4. Describe the characteristics of a high performance team.
5. How can managers help individuals become effective team members?
6. Chart the key contemporary issues regarding groups in organizations and why each is important.

I. THE POPULARITY OF TEAMS
A. Introduction
1. Two decades ago
2. Today,
3. The current popularity of teams
4. As organizations restructure themselves
5. Teams can serve

B. What Are the Stages of Team Development?
1. Most teams
2. There's a general pattern that describes how most teams evolve.
   a) See Exhibit 9-1.
3. Forming is
4. The storming stage is
5. Norming stage is
6. The fourth stage is performing
7. For temporary teams, there is an adjourning stage.
8. Some researchers argue that
9. Under some conditions,
10. Teams do not
11. It is better to think of these stages as

C. Aren't Work Groups and Work Teams the Same?
1. A group is
2. A work group is
3. A work team

    4. Exhibit 9-2 highlights the main differences between work groups and work teams.
    5. Management is looking for
    6. Nothing inherently magical in the creation of work teams guarantees

II. TYPES OF WORK TEAMS
  A. See Exhibit 9-3

  B. What Is a Functional Team?
    1. Functional teams are
    2. Issues such as
    3. Functional teams are

  C. How Does a Problem-Solving Team Operate?
    1. Twenty years ago
    2. One of the most widely practiced applications was
      a) These are work teams
      b) They meet regularly to
      c) They assume responsibility for
      d) These teams are

  D. What Is a Self-Managed Work Team?
    1. A self-managed work team is
    2. This kind of team
    3. Fully self-managed work teams
    4. As a result,

  E. How Do Cross-Functional Teams Operate?
    1. This type of team consists
    2. Cross-functional teams are
    3. But cross-functional teams can be
      a) The early stages of development
      b) This difficulty with diversity
    4. As team members become more familiar with one another

  F. Are Virtual Teams a Reality Today?
    1. A virtual team is
    2. A virtual team allows
    3. Team members

III. CHARACTERISTICS OF HIGH-PERFORMANCE WORK TEAMS
  A. Introduction
    1. Primary characteristics of high-performance work teams are summarized in Exhibit 9-4.
    2. High-performance work teams
    3. Effective teams are
      a) They have
      b) They are capable of
      c) High-performing teams have members who
    4. Effective teams are characterized by
      a) Members believe in
      b) Members of an effective team exhibit

       c) Members redefine themselves to include
       d) Unified commitment is characterized by
    5. Effective teams are characterized by
       a) Members convey
       b) Their communication is also characterized by
    6. Effective teams tend to be
       a) Team members must possess
       b) The members have to be able to
    7. Effective leaders can
       a) Leaders help
       b) They demonstrate
       c) They increase
       d) Effective team leaders
    8. The final condition necessary
       a) The team should be provided with

IV. TURNING INDIVIDUALS INTO TEAM PLAYERS
A. Introduction
    1. Some individuals prefer
    2. In some organizations, work environments are such that
    3. Creating teams in such an environment may
    4. Teams fit well with countries that score

B. What Are the Management Challenges of Creating Team Players?
    1. Employees' success, when they are part of teams, is a function of
    2. To perform well as team members, individuals
    3. The challenge of creating team players will be greatest where
    4. In contrast, the challenge for management is less demanding when
    5. The challenge of forming teams will also be less in

C. What Roles Do Team Members Play?
    1. High-performing work teams
    2. There are nine potential roles that work team members often can "play."
       a) See Exhibit 9-5.
    3. Creator-innovators are
    4. Explorer-promoters like to
    5. Assessor-developers have
    6. Thruster-organizers like to
    7. And, somewhat like thruster-organizers, concluder-producers are
    8. Controller-inspectors have
    9. Upholder-maintainers hold
    10. Reporter-advisers are
    11. The Linkers overlap
    12. If forced to, most individuals can perform in any of these roles.
       a) Most have two or three they strongly prefer.
    13. Managers need to select team members

D. How Can a Manager Shape Team Behavior?
    1. The three most popular ways include

E. What Role Does Selection Play?
1. When hiring team members
    a) Some job applicants
    b) If team skills are
    c) A candidate who has some basic team skills but

F. Can We Train Individuals to Be Team Players?
1. Performing well in a team involves
2. People who were raised on
3. Training specialists can
4. The workshops offered
5. Outside consultants can provide

G. What Role Do Rewards Play in Shaping Team Players?
1. The organization's reward system
2. Lockheed Martin's Space Launch Systems has
3. Promotions, pay raises, and other forms of recognition should be
4. Individual contribution is balanced
5. Managers cannot forget
6. Work teams provide

H. How Can a Manager Reinvigorate a Mature Team?
1. Effective teams can become
    a)
    b)
    c)
    d)
2. Mature teams,
    a)
    b)
3. What a manager can do to reinvigorate mature teams, four suggestions.
    a) See Exhibit 9-6.
    b)
    c)
    d)
    e)

V. CONTEMPORARY TEAM ISSUES
A. Why Are Teams Central to Continuous Process Improvement Programs?
1. The essence of continuous improvement is
2. As one author put it
3. All such techniques and processes require
4. Teams provide
5. Ford began its continuous improvement efforts
6. The teams should be
    a)
    b)
    c)
    d)
    e)
7. At Allegiance HealthCare,

Chapter 9- Understanding Work Teams

B. How Does Workforce Diversity Affect Teams?
1. Managing diversity on teams is
2. Diversity typically provides
3. The strongest case for diversity is
   a) Heterogeneous teams
   b) The lack of a common perspective usually means
4. The positive contribution that diversity makes
5. Expect the value-added component of diverse teams to
6. Studies tell us that members of cohesive teams
7. So here is a potential negative of diversity.
   a)
   b)
   c)

REVIEW QUESTIONS

1. Outline the five stages groups move through in their evolution and what problems they might encounter.
   Answer – Pages 289-290

2. Compare and contrast self-managed and cross-functional teams; and virtual and face-to-face teams.
   Answer – Pages 291-294

3. Review the characteristics of high-performance work teams explain the role of each in fostering effectiveness.
   Answer – Pages 295-297

4. What challenges do managers face in converting individuals into team players?
   Answer – Pages 297-298

5. List and explain the various roles individuals play in groups?
   Answer – Pages 298-299

6. How can managers share and direct team behavior?
   Answer – Pages 299-301

7. In what ways can management invigorate stagnant teams?
   Answer – Pages 301-302

8. What part do teams play in continuous improvement?
   Answer – Pages 302-303

STUDY QUIZ
Multiple Choice Questions

1. Teams have become popular in organizations for a number of reasons, including:
   a) they provide job security for employees during times of downsizing and reorganization.
   b) a growing acceptance of their presence by union leadership.
   c) being a better way to utilize employee skills and create organizational flexibility.
   d) all of these.

2. If members of a team accept the existence of the team but resist its constraints on their individuality, then it is most likely this team is in the _____ stage of team development.
    a) forming
    b) storming
    c) norming
    d) performing

3. A _____ team is often composed of a manager and the employees in the manager's work unit. Decision making, leadership, etc., are relatively clear and simple, and the team may be used to address specific issues or problems within the work unit.
    a) functional
    b) problem-solving
    c) cross-functional
    d) virtual

4. Joanne is a member of a _____ team. They do not have a supervisor, they schedule and evaluate their own work, and even select their own team members.
    a) functional
    b) problem-solving
    c) virtual
    d) self-managed

5. _____ are an effective way to allow employees from different areas within a company to share information, develop new ideas, and solve problems. However, they are often difficult to manage, and the storming stage can be very time-consuming.
    a) Functional teams
    b) Problem-solving teams
    c) Cross-functional teams
    d) Self-managed teams

6. High-performing teams are often characterized by:
    a) relatively ambiguous goals that force the team to cooperate in clarifying and reshaping them.
    b) a belief in the integrity, character, and ability of team members.
    c) a strong rigidity in roles and skills of the individual members.
    d) high commitment to each other but not to the group.

7. A key skill high-performing team members need in order to maintain flexibility is:
    a) negotiating skills.
    b) high-self monitoring skills.
    c) strong self-esteem.
    d) the ability to follow.

8. When a firm initiates or uses teams, a significant accompanying change in organizational culture is:
    a) a discounting of the importance of leadership and leadership opportunities.
    b) an elimination of promotional opportunities in the management ranks.
    c) the cessation of the use of MBO and goal-theory as motivational techniques.
    d) that employee success depends on team performance, not individual performance.

9. The challenge of forming work teams would be less in which of the following countries?
   a) Mexico.
   b) the United States
   c) Great Britain.
   d) Australia.

10. The ____ in a team likes to take new ideas and champion them.
    a) creator-innovator
    b) explorer-promoter
    c) thruster-organizer
    d) none of these individuals or roles

11. This role can be assumed by any team member who plays any other role, and it tends to overlap all other roles.
    a) concluder-producer
    b) upholder-maintainer
    c) reporter-advisor
    d) linker

12. When shaping individual's behavior to help them be more effective team members it is important to:
    a) hire people with an ability to cooperate with others.
    b) provide training in negotiation, conflict resolution, communication, etc.
    c) offer a percentage of their rewards in terms of team performance and team goals.
    d) do all of these things.

13. Successful teams:
    a) continue to be successful and generally stable in their development stage.
    b) can become stagnant, victims of their own success.
    c) generally are self-directed and do not have either an appointed or emergent leader.
    d) are characterized by all of these elements.

14. Teams are often very important to continuous process improvement programs because:
    a) employee participation is central to such processes.
    b) they are effective ways to coopt individuals into cooperating with the process changes.
    c) such use of teams gives managers greater leverage in pushing through changes.
    d) these types of teams promote homogeneity, common goals, and group thought.

15. Diversity on teams:
    a) generally results in the eventual disintegration of the team.
    b) fosters creative and unique solutions to problems.
    c) makes such teams less difficult to manage, contrary to managers' expectations.
    d) comes naturally in today's workforce and takes little management effort.

True/False Questions
1. Today, teams are used in almost all organizations in business.

2. Once a team moves through the five stages of development, it stabilizes and does not experience much change.

3. A work group is a work unit that creates a positive synergy through the coordination of effort.

4. Problem-solving teams are small groups of employees from the same department who meet regularly to discuss quality improvement, increased efficiency, and the work environment.

5. A cross-functional team is a permanent group of people from different levels in an organization and different departments who work together to manage a work process.

6. The primary difference between a virtual team and other forms of teams is that the virtual team members are not physically located together in the same geographic area.

7. The concept of unified commitment identifies the loyalty and dedication group members have toward the group and each other in a high-performance team.

8. In high-performing teams, leadership is relatively unimportant.

9. National culture has little impact on team formation or function as corporate culture is far more influential in team situations.

10. The team member role of creator-innovator is that role of initiating ideas and concepts, and these individuals actually prefer to work at their own pace and in their own way, a seeming contradiction for a group member role.

11. Controller-inspectors in a group hold strong convictions about the way things should be done, and this is the role that overlaps all the other roles, tying things together.

12. When shaping team behavior, the selection process is probably the most important way a manager can shape effective team behavior.

13. Only those individuals who come from collectivist cultures can be trained to become effective team members.

14. If a team has a record of success, there is little chance that it will become stagnant or need reinvigoration.

15. Providing training, reminding the team it is not unique, etc., are effective ways to reinvigorate mature stagnant teams.

Answers to Chapter 9 Study Quiz

Multiple Choice (Page - Answer)

1. c-289	6. b-295	11. d-299
2. b-290	7. a-296	12. d-300
3. a-291	8. d-297	13. b-301
4. d-292	9. a-298	14. a-302
5. c-293	10. b-299	15. b-303

True/False

1. T-288	6. T-294	11. F-299
2. F-289	7. T-295	12. T-299
3. F-290	8. F-296	13. F-300
4. T-292	9. F-297	14. F-301
5. F-293	10. T-298	15. T-302

CHAPTER 10 - MOTIVATING AND REWARDING EMPLOYEES

LEARNING OUTCOMES

After reading this chapter, you should be able to:
1. Describe the motivation process.
2. Define needs.
3. Explain the hierarchy of needs theory.
4. Differentiate Theory X from Theory Y.
5. Explain the motivational implications of the motivation-hygiene theory.
6. Describe the motivational implications of equity theory.
7. Explain the key relationships in expectancy theory.
8. Describe how managers can design individual jobs to maximize employee performance.
9. Describe the effect of workforce diversity on motivational practices.

Use the Outline to Guide Your Note Taking from the Text

Considerations as you read

As you read and take notes, think about these questions; they will help you organize your study notes.
1. Describe the factors that shape individual motivation.
2. Explain the assumptions underlying McGregor and Herzberg's theories of motivation.
3. How can McClelland's theory of motivation help managers to manage people?
4. What are the practical implications of equity theory for organizational behavior?
5. How does job design influence worker motivation?
6. In what ways can a manager use his/her knowledge of expectancy theory to manage his/her employees?
7. Diagram and explain the text's integrated model of motivation.

I. MOTIVATION AND INDIVIDUAL NEEDS
A. Definitions
1. Many incorrectly view motivation as a personal trait.
2. Motivation is
   a) Individuals differ
   b) An individual's motivation
3. We'll define motivation as
4. Three key elements
   a)
   b)
   c)
   d) This is depicted in Exhibit 10-1.
5. A need
   a) An unsatisfied need
   b) These drives generate
6. We can say that motivated employees are
   a) To relieve this tension
   b) The greater the tension
7. Inherent in our definition of motivation is

II. EARLY THEORIES OF MOTIVATION
A. Introduction
1. In the 1950s, three specific theories were formulated.
   a) Now considered questionably valid, are probably still the best-known explanations for employee motivation.
   b)
   c)
   d)
2. More valid explanations of motivation have been developed; students should know these theories because:
   a) They represent the foundation from which contemporary theories grew.
   b) Practicing managers regularly use these theories and their terminology.

B. What Is Maslow's Hierarchy of Needs Theory?
1. The best-known theory of motivation.
2. Within every human, being there exists
   a)
   b)
   c)
   d)
   e)
3. As each need is
   a) See Exhibit 10-2.
4. No need is
5. To motivate, you need to understand
6. Widely recognized
7. Research does not
8. Maslow had

C. What Is McGregor's Theory X and Theory Y?
1. Douglas McGregor proposed two distinct views of the nature of human beings.
   a) A basically negative view
   b) A basically positive view
2. McGregor held that
   a) See Exhibit 10-3.
3. Theory X assumes that
4. Theory Y assumes that
5. McGregor held to the belief that
6. There is

D. What Is Herzberg's Motivation-Hygiene Theory?
1. An individual's relation
2. Herzberg investigated the question
   a) Exhibit 10-4 represents Herzberg's findings.
3. He concluded that
   a) Intrinsic factors
   b) When dissatisfied
4. The opposite of satisfaction is not
   a) Removing dissatisfying characteristics
   b) Exhibit 10-5

    5. Managers who
       a) The factors that eliminate job dissatisfaction
       b) To motivate people on their jobs
    6. The criticisms of the theory include
    7. Much of the enthusiasm for enriching jobs

III. CONTEMPORARY THEORIES OF MOTIVATION

A. "State-of-the-art" Explanations of Employee Motivation.

B. What Is McClelland's Three-Needs Theory?
    1. David McClelland and others have proposed the three-needs theory.
    2. Need for achievement (nAch)
       a)
       b)
       c)
       d)
       e)
    3. Need for power (nPow)
       a)
       b)
    4. Need for affiliation (nAff)
       a)
       b)
       c)

C. How Do Inputs and Outcomes Influence Motivation?
    1. Employees make comparisons.
    2. There is considerable evidence that
    3. Developed by J. Stacey Adams, equity theory says that
       a) See Exhibit 10-6.
       b) If they perceive
       c) If the ratios are unequal
    4. The referent is
    5. There are three referent categories
       a) Other includes
       b) The system considers
       c) Self refers to
    6. The choice of a particular set of referents is related to
    7. When employees perceive an inequity, they might
       a)
       b)
       c)
       d)
       e)
    8. Individuals are concerned with
    9. On the basis of one's inputs, such as
    10. An imbalance in inputs-outcomes ratio
    11. The theory establishes the four propositions relating to inequitable pay.
       a) Listed in Exhibit 10-7.
    12. Whenever employees perceive inequity

13. Equity theory is not without problems.
    a)
    b)
    c)
    d)
14. Equity theory

D. Does Job Design Influence Motivation?
1. What differentiates one job from another?
2. The job characteristics model (JCM)
    a) Skill variety.
    b) Task identity.
    c) Task significance.
    d) Autonomy.
    e) Feedback.
3. The core dimensions can be combined into
4. Exhibit 10-8 offers examples of job activities that rate high and low for each characteristic.
5. Exhibit 10-9 presents the model.
6. Individuals with a high growth need are
7. Research on the JCM has found that
8. Jobs that possess autonomy
9. Jobs that provide feedback
10. JCM says that

E. What Does the JCM Tell Us?
1. Jobs will score high on motivating potential if
2. They must also be high on
3. The job characteristics model
4. Most of the evidence supports
5. But there is still considerable debate around
    a) There is some question whether
    b) The strength of an individual's growth needs
6. Other variables may be
7. One should be cautious in

F. Where Does This Leave Us?
1. The JCM provides
2. People who work on jobs with high core job dimensions are
3. Job dimensions operate through the psychological states

G. Why Is Expectancy Theory Considered a Comprehensive Theory of Motivation?
1. The most comprehensive explanation of motivation is Victor Vroom's expectancy theory.
2. It states that
3. It includes three variables or relationships.
    a)
    b)
    c)
4. It can be summed up in the following questions:
    a)
    b)
    c)

H. How Does Expectancy Theory Work?
1. Exhibit 10-10 shows a very simple version of expectancy theory.
2. The strength of a person's motivation
3. If this goal is achieved
4. If so
   a) First
   b) Second,
   c) Third,
   d) Fourth,

I. How Can Expectancy Theory Be Applied?
1. A classroom analogy as an illustration.
2. Most students prefer
3. Consider that five weeks into
4. You studied hard
5. Well, the results of that first examination are in.
   a)
   b)
   c)
   d)
6. Suddenly,
7. Exhibit 10-10 can help us understand this situation.
   a) Studying for MNGT 301
   b) The attractiveness of the outcome
   c) The performance-reward linkage is
8. Another possible demotivating force
   a)
   b)
9. Summarize the issues surrounding the theory.
   a) First
   b) Second
   c) Third,
   d) Finally,
10. The individual's perception of the outcome will determine the effort expended.

J. How Can We Integrate the Contemporary Theories of Motivation?
1. There is a tendency to view
2. Exhibit 10-11 presents a model that integrates much of what we know about motivation.
3. The goals-effort loop is
   a) Expectancy theory predicts
   b) Need theories tells us that
4. The model considers the need for
5. Finally, we can see the JCM in this exhibit
   a) First
   b) Second

IV. CONTEMPORARY ISSUES IN MOTIVATION
A. What Is the Key to Motivating a Diverse Workforce?
1. Flexibility is
2. Studies show that

3. The opportunity to learn
4. Employees have different personal needs and goals
5. Motivating a diverse workforce also means that
   a) The theories of motivation
6. These theories need to be modified for different cultures.
   a) The self-interest concept is
   b) These motivation theories should be applicable to
   c) In more collectivist nations
7. The need-for-achievement concept also
   a) It presupposes the existence of
   b) These characteristics would exclude
8. Several recent studies
   a) Motivational techniques were shown to be
9. Managers must change

B. Should Employees Be Paid for Performance or Time on the Job?
1. What's in it for me?
2. People do what they do to
3. Pay is
4. Pay-for-performance programs are
5. These forms of pay reflect
6. Performance-based compensation is
7. Pay-for-performance programs are
8. The growing popularity can be explained
9. Making some or all of a worker's pay conditional on performance measures
   a) However, if
   b) On the cost-savings side
10. A recent extension of this concept is called competency-based compensation.
    a) It pays and rewards employees on the basis of
    b) Pay levels are established on the basis of
    c) Pay increases in a competency-based system are awarded for

C. How Can Managers Motivate Minimum-Wage Employees?
1. One of the toughest motivational challenges facing many managers today is
2. One trap many managers fall into is
3. In motivating minimum-wage employees, managers should
   a)
   b)
4. The power of praise
5. In service industries, successful companies are
   a) If we use the JCM to examine this change, we can see that

D. What's Different in Motivating Professional and Technical Employees?
1. Professional and technical employees are
   a)
   b)
   c)
2. Money and promotions into management typically are

3. Job challenge tends to be
   a)
   b)
   c)
   d)
4. Managers should provide
   a)
   b)
   c)
   d)
5. They put a high value on
6. An increasing number of companies are
7. These allow employees to

E. How Can Flexible Work Options Influence Motivation?
1. Example—Barry Cunningham is the classic "morning person."
2. Many employees continue to work
3. A number of scheduling options
4. A compressed workweek is
5. Flextime is

F. Can Employees Share Jobs?
1. Job sharing is
2. Job sharing is
3. Job sharing allows
4. Telecommuting
   a)
   b)
   c)
   d)
   e)

REVIEW QUESTIONS
1. Describe how needs, effort, drives, etc., shape motivation.
   Answer – Pages 312-314

2. Chart the premises underlying Theory X and Theory Y.
   Answer – Pages 315-316

3. How might a manager use Herzberg's motivation-hygiene theory to manage employee behavior?
   Answer – Pages 316-317

4. Describe three-needs theory.
   Answer – Pages 317-318

5. What are some of the possible consequences of employees' perceiving an inequity between their inputs and outcomes and those of others?
   Answer – Pages 318-321

6. Outline the elements of the JCM model, and explain how the motivating potential score is calculated. How can managers use the JCM model?
   Answer – Pages 321-323

7. Discuss the three variables upon which expectancy theory is built. How can this theory be used to motivate employees?
   Answer – Pages 324-327

8. What are the contemporary issues regarding motivation and motivation theory?
   Answer – Pages 328-329

9. In what circumstances should a firm use pay-for-performance programs to motivate employees? What are the drawbacks of such a compensation system?
   Answer – Pages 330-331

10. What are the unique challenges of motivating a minimum wage workforce?
    Answer – Pages 331-332

11. How can managers use flexible work options to motivate employees?
    Answer – Pages 333-335

STUDY QUIZ
Multiple Choice Questions
1. Todd and Nick are discussing the willingness of their employees to exert a high degree of effort to win their company's sales contest. Todd and Nick are essentially discussing the concept of:
   a) needs.
   b) wants.
   c) motivation.
   d) cooperation.

2. It is the assumption of _____ theory of motivation that physiological needs dominate the individual employee and are the ones a manager should focus on when seeking to motivate.
   a) Maslow's hierarchy of needs
   b) McGregor's Theory X
   c) McClelland's three needs
   d) Herzberg's motivation-hygiene

3. Jacob and Xaikiya are both highly motivated by the need to excel and achieve in terms of the standards they set for themselves. In terms of McClelland's three-needs theory, they would be classified as having a high need for:
   a) affiliation.
   b) success.
   c) power.
   d) achievement.

4. The motivational theory that argues employees evaluate their rewards in terms of their effort and if that "ratio" is comparable to what others do and receive it is known as:
   a) expectancy theory.
   b) McClelland's three-need theory.
   c) equity theory.
   d) absolute reward theory.

5. Which of the following is true regarding employee motivation in terms of equity theory?
   a) Overrewarded hourly workers will produce more than equitably paid employees.
   b) Overrewarded workers paid piece-rate will produce more and better quality.
   c) Underrewarded hourly workers will produce more and better quality units than equitably paid workers.
   d) Piece rate workers who are underpaid will produce fewer but higher quality units than equitably paid workers.

6. For a job to be high on the motivational scale according to JCM, a job must:
   a) be high on all five factors to be highly motivating.
   b) part of a employee empowerment effort or self-managed team to be highly motivating.
   c) provide an opportunity to socialize and create a sense of community to be motivating.
   d) be high on skill variety, task identity, or task significance.

7. Ultimately, individual effort, in terms of expectancy theory, is linked to:
   a) the leadership the individual receives from his/her manager.
   b) an individual goals.
   c) the goals and objectives of the organization.
   d) the size of the reward.

8. If you are thinking about expectancy theory in seeking to motivate your employees, you would most likely accept the idea that:
   a) perceptions of the reward, not the actual reward, are key to employee motivation.
   b) rewards or payoffs are not as important as your management style and the way employees are treated.
   c) fairness is central to motivation.
   d) the attractiveness of a reward is relatively unimportant in relation to its size.

9. In seeking to translate motivation theory into other cultures, research shows that:
   a) no motivation theory is translatable due to the American bias in these theories.
   b) self-interest is a fundamental assumption and will work only in cultures similar to the United States.
   c) none of these theories works well in collectivist cultures.
   d) all of these are true.

10. Performance-based compensation programs:
    a) are in sharp decline due to their expense.
    b) being replaced by competency-based compensation programs.
    c) are gaining in popularity with nearly 80% of surveyed companies using them.
    d) work very well in collectivist cultures and are one of the few theories that transcends culture.

11. Seeking to motivate your minimum-wage restaurant employees, you might consider:
    a) using an employee recognition program.
    b) providing more challenging work.
    c) focusing on money.
    d) none of these.

12. Which of the following would be an effective way to motivate professional and technical workers?
    a) Promotional opportunities.
    b) Employee recognition programs.
    c) High salaries.
    d) Challenging work.

13. The flexible work option that has the unfortunate drawbacks of decreased worker productivity, decrease in the quality of customer service, and an underutilization of equipment is:
    a) job sharing.
    b) compressed workweek.
    c) flextime.
    d) telecommuting.

14. Your company wants to help clerical employees avoid the rush hour traffic, provide some flexibility in their work schedules, while reducing absenteeism. Their best choice of flexible work schedule is:
    a) job sharing.
    b) compressed workweek.
    c) flextime.
    d) telecommuting.

15. The flexible work schedule option that may cause employees to feel isolated from their company and fellow workers, may increase their distraction while working, and that makes it more difficult for managers to supervise their work efforts is:
    a) job sharing.
    b) compressed workweek.
    c) flextime.
    d) telecommuting.

True/False Questions

1. Motivation is simply an internal state that makes certain outcomes appear attractive.

2. If a manager wants to use Maslow's hierarchy of needs as a motivational tool, it is essential that he/she know which level each employee is in his/her work unit.

3. In Herzberg's motivation-hygiene theory, intrinsic factors are those which actually motivate higher peformance in workers, rather than extrinsic factors.

4. In equity theory, the referent is the objective standard by which an individual evaluates his/her performance when evaluating how well he/she is doing.

5. In the JCM model, task identify is simply the degree to which a job requires the completion of a whole identifiable piece of work.

6. Autonomy in the JCM provides the critical psychological state of an experience of meaningfulness of the work one does.

7. In terms of expectancy theory, the potential outcome for an effort must be attractive to the employee for it to be motivating.

8. If the performance-reward linkage is weak, individual effort will be weak, regardless of how attractive the reward is to the employee, according to expectancy theory.

9. Key to motivating a diverse workforce is treating everyone the same.

10. Like other management theories, almost none of the work in motivational theory is translatable into other cultures ,due to its heavy American, western-bias.

11. A competency-based compensation program essentially rewards employees for learning more about their job and other jobs rather than for actually improving their productivity.

12. When working with minimum-wage employees, managers should remember that money is almost always a motivator.

13. With professional and technical employees, salary and promotion are actually poor motivators.

14. Flextime is a work program that permits employees to either work a shorter week or to share a job with another individual.

15. Nearly 16 million people are involved in telecommuting.

Answers to Chapter 10 Study Quiz

Multiple Choice (Page - Answer)

1. c-313	6. d-322	11. a-331
2. b-315	7. b-324	12. d-332
3. d-317	8. a-327	13. b-333
4. c-318	9. b-329	14. c-334
5. a-320	10. c-330	15. d-335

True/False

1. F-313	6. F-323	11. T-330
2. T-314	7. T-324	12. F-331
3. T-316	8. T-326	13. T-332
4. F-318	9. F-328	14. F-334
5. T-321	10. F-329	15. T-335

CHAPTER 11 - LEADERSHIP AND TRUST

LEARNING OUTCOMES
After reading this chapter, you should be able to:
1. Define the term leader and explain the difference between managers and leaders.
2. Summarize the conclusions of trait theories of leadership.
3. Describe the Fiedler contingency model.
4. Summarize the path-goal model of leadership.
5. Explain situational leadership.
6. Identify the qualities that characterize charismatic leaders.
7. Describe the skills that visionary leaders exhibit.
8. Explain the four specific roles of effective team leaders.
9. Identify the five dimensions of trust.

Use the Outline to Guide Your Note Taking from the Text

Considerations as you read

As you read and take notes think about these questions they will help you organize your study notes.
1. Is there a real difference between managers and leaders?
2. Can you explain the value of each of the various theories of leadership?
3. What was the importance of the Ohio State and University of Michigan studies to later leadership theories?
4. What are the drawbacks of the leadership theories prior to the emerging and contemporary leadership theories?
5. What do the contemporaries theories add to our understanding of leadership?
6. What is trust?
7. What type of trust do you have with the following: your family, the professor, your class mates, your significant other? Why? How would you take it to a higher level of trust?

I. MANAGERS VERSUS LEADERS
A. Introduction
   1. Managers are
   2. Leaders
   3. We believe that all managers
   4. However, not all leaders

II. TRAIT THEORIES OF LEADERSHIP
A. Introduction
   1. The average person's definition of leadership
   2. If the concept of traits were to prove valid
   3. Research efforts at isolating these traits
   4. Attempts to identify traits consistently associated with leadership
   5. Explanations based solely on traits
   6. A major movement

III. BEHAVIORAL THEORIES OF LEADERSHIP

A. Introduction

1. It was hoped that the behavioral theories
2. We shall briefly review three of the most popular studies:
   a) Kurt Lewin's studies at the University of Iowa.
   b) the Ohio State group.
   c) the University of Michigan studies.

B. Are There Identifiable Leadership Behaviors?

1. One of the first studies; Kurt Lewin and his associates at the University of Iowa
2. Which one of the three leadership styles was most effective?
3. Tannenbaum and Schmidt developed
4. Tannenbaum and Schmidt proposed that
5. Managers should

C. What Was the Importance of the Ohio State Studies?

1. The most comprehensive and replicated of the behavioral theories.
2. These studies sought to
3. Beginning with over 1,000 dimensions
4. Research found that
5. However, leader behavior characterized as high on initiating structure
6. Other studies found that high consideration was

D. What Were the Leadership Dimensions of the University of Michigan Studies?

1. Two dimensions of leadership behavior
2. Employee-oriented leaders
3. The production-oriented leaders
4. The Michigan researchers

E. What Is the Managerial Grid?

1. A two-dimensional view of leadership style developed by Robert Blake and Jane Mouton.
2. The grid, depicted in Exhibit 11-3, has
3. The grid shows
4. Blake and Mouton concluded that
5. The grid offers

F. What Did the Behavioral Theories Teach Us about Leadership?

1. Behavioral researchers have had very little success in
2. What was missing was

IV. CONTINGENCY THEORIES OF LEADERSHIP

A. Introduction

1. Predicting leadership success
2. Leadership effectiveness depended on

B. What Is the Fiedler Model?

1. The first comprehensive contingency model for leadership.
2. Effective group performance depends on
3. Fiedler developed an instrument,
4. Fiedler believed that an individual's basic leadership style is a key factor.
5. What you say about others

     6. Fiedler argued that leadership style is innate

     7. It is necessary to match the leader with

     8. Leader-member relations

     9. Task structure

     10. Position power

     11. The next step is to

C. How Does Path-Goal Theory Operate?

     1. One of the most respected approaches to leadership is path-goal theory.

     2. Developed by

     3. The essence of the theory

     4. A leader's behavior is

     5. A leader's behavior is motivational to

     6. House identified four leadership behaviors.

     7. The directive leader

     8. The supportive leader

     9. The participative leader

     10. The achievement-oriented leader

     11. In contrast to Fiedler, House

     12. Exhibit 11-5

     13. Research to validate path-goal predictions

D. What Is the Leader-Participation Model?

     1. Back in 1973, Victor Vroom and Phillip Yetton developed a leader-participation model.

     2. Recognizing that task structures

     3. The model was a decision tree

     4. The new model retains

     5. Research testing the original leader-participation model

E. How Does Situational Leadership Operate?

     1. Paul Hersey and Kenneth Blanchard developed the leadership model.

     2. A contingency theory that focuses on the followers.

     3. Why focus on the followers

     4. The term readiness refers to

     5. The leader-follower relationship

     6. The most effective behavior depends on

     7. SLT has an intuitive appeal.

     8. Research efforts to test and support the theory have

V. EMERGING APPROACHES TO LEADERSHIP

A. What Is Charismatic Leadership Theory?

     1. Charismatic leadership theory is an extension of attribution theory.

     2. Several authors have attempted to identify personal characteristics of the charismatic leader.

     3. There is an increasing body of research

B. What is Visionary Leadership?

     1. Visionary leadership goes

     2. Visionary leadership is the ability to

     3. A vision differs from other forms of direction setting in several ways

     4. The key properties of a vision seem to be

5. Examples of visions
    a) Rupert Murdoch
    b) Mary Kay Ash's
    c) Michael Dell
6. What skills do visionary leaders exhibit?

C. How Do Transactional Leaders Differ from Transformational Leaders?
1. Most of the leadership theories presented in this chapter
2. Transformational leaders
3. Transformational leadership is built on
4. The evidence supporting the superiority of transformational leadership
5. The overall evidence indicates that

VI. CONTEMPORARY LEADERSHIP ISSUES
A. What Is Team Leadership?
1. Leadership is increasingly taking place within a team context.
2. As teams grow in popularity
3. Many leaders are not equipped to handle the change to teams.
4. One prominent consultant estimates
5. The challenge for most managers is
6. A study of 20 organizations that had reorganized themselves around teams found
7. A more meaningful way to describe
8. First, team leaders are
9. Second, team leaders are
10. Third, team leaders are
11. Finally, team leaders are

B. Does National Cultural Affect Leadership?
1. National culture is
2. National culture affects
3. Leaders choice of styles is
    a) Korean leaders
    b) Arab leaders
    c) Japanese leaders
    d) Scandinavian and Dutch leaders
4. Most leadership theories
5. As a guide for adjusting your leadership style consider

C. Is Leadership Always Important?
1. Data from numerous studies demonstrate that
2. Certain individual, job, and organizational variables
3. Characteristics of employees such as
4. Jobs that are inherently
5. Organizational characteristics as

VII. BUILDING TRUST: THE ESSENCE OF LEADERSHIP
A. What is Trust?
1. Trust is
2. Trust is a
3. Trust involves
4. What are the key dimensions that underlie the concept of trust?

B. Why Is Trust One Foundation of Leadership
1. Trust appears to be
2. Part of the leader's task has been
3. When followers trust a leader, they
4. Honesty consistently
5. Now, more than ever, managerial and leadership effectiveness depends on
6. In times of change and instability,
7. Moreover, contemporary management practices such as

C. What Are the Three Types of Trust
1. Deterrence-based Trust
2. Knowledge-based Trust
3. Identification-based Trust

REVIEW QUESTIONS

1. Why were trait studies important, what were they trying to discover, and why don't they work?
   Answer – Page 345

2. What do behavioral leadership studies add to our understanding of leadership? What were their weaknesses?
   Answer – Pages 345-347

3. The Ohio State studies added what dimensions to the study and understanding of leadership? How were the University of Michigan studies different?
   Answer – Pages 348-349

4. What is the managerial grid?
   Answer – Page 349

5. Compare and contrast the following contingency leadership theories: Fielder's LPC, path-goal theory, and Blanchard and Hersey's SLT.
   Answer – Pages 350-357

6. Explain charismatic leadership theory. What are its strengths and its dangers?
   Answer – Pages 358-359

7. Compare and contrast charismatic, visionary, and transformational leadership theories.
   Answer – Pages 358-361

8. Explain the differences between transformational and transactional leadership.
   Answer – Pages 360-361

9. How is team leadership different from other forms of leadership?
   Answer – Pages 361-363

10. What is trust? How do you develop higher levels of trust?
    Answer – Pages 365-368

STUDY QUIZ
Multiple Choice Questions

1. The primary difference between leaders and managers is:
   a) leaders have position power, managers are referent power.
   b) managers emerge into their roles through the ranks, leaders are appointed.
   c) leaders influence others and have managerial ability, managers influence through position.
   d) all leaders are managers and all managers are leaders.

2. If Brian is looking for leadership in job candidates by examining their drive, honesty and integrity, desire to lead, etc., he is approaching leadership from a _____ leadership theory perspective.
   a) trait
   b) behavior
   c) situational
   d) contingency

3. When you train managers in leadership by stressing their ability to establish structure for employees and themselves and their relationship with those employees you are training them from a _____ leadership perspective.
   a) behavioral
   b) Ohio State University
   c) managerial grid
   d) Fiedler LPC

4. Behavior leadership theories have been important for what they've taught us, which is:
   a) that we can define leadership behaviors if we have clear, thorough job descriptions.
   b) there are certain characteristics to look forward which show an orientation toward leadership in the perspective employee.
   c) nothing, like trait studies, behavioral studies were largely a wasted effort.
   d) leadership studies were missing a consideration of the context in which leadership was exercised.

5. The basic idea behind Fiedler's LPC-based theory of leadership is that:
   a) what a manager says about others tells more about his/her leadership theory than anything else.
   b) a manager's orientation toward task and relationship determines his/her leadership style.
   c) it is the leader's personality or ability to cast a vision that determines his/her effectiveness as a leader.
   d) none of these.

6. The essence of _____ leadership theory is that the leader gives his/her followers the direction and support necessary to set goals compatible with the organization and to achieve them.
   a) transformational
   b) managerial grid
   c) contingency
   d) path-goal

7. Path-goal leadership theory closely parallels _____ leadership theory.
   a) Blanchard and Hersey's SLT
   b) managerial grid
   c) the Ohio State
   d) visionary

8. A leadership theory that focuses on participation in decision making and that helps managers determine how much participation to allow employees to have in certain types of decisions is:
   a) transactional leadership theory.
   b) leader-participation model.
   c) situational leadership theory.
   d) team leadership theory.

9. Situational Leadership theory rests primarily on which element?
   a) The readiness of the follower to perform.
   b) The type of decision that needs to be made.
   c) The attributions of the leader.
   d) The vision of the leader.

10. Charismatic leadership theory is an extension of:
    a) attribution theory.
    b) behavioral theory.
    c) situational leadership theory.
    d) transformational leadership theory.

11. Key to visionary leadership is:
    a) the characteristics of the leader.
    b) the ability to explain a vision to others.
    c) the context within which the leadership is exercised.
    d) the nature of the followers.

12. Team leadership differs from other leadership theories in that:
    a) it is the personality of the manager that determines his/her success.
    b) the context of the leadership effort has no effect on what the leader should do.
    c) the manager must take more of a role of facilitator.
    d) it involves more participation than any other leadership theory.

13. Leadership theories translate best in which of the following countries/cultures?
    a) Asian.
    b) European.
    c) Middle-Eastern.
    d) None of these.

14. Trust is built on several dimensions, including:
    a) intelligence.
    b) willingness to work.
    c) integrity.
    d) ability to perform.

15. _____ is foundational to all forms of leadership.
    a) Personality
    b) Context
    c) Followership
    d) Trust

True/False Questions

1. While trait leadership theories were largely a failure, they have identified six traits that seem to be consistently linked to leadership.

2. In terms of behavioral leadership, the least effective leadership style across most situations was the laissez-faire style.

3. The University of Michigan leadership studies strongly favored task or production oriented leaders.

4. The managerial grid by Blake and Mouton was built on the work of Blanchard and Hersey SLT.

5. Fiedler's LPC theory takes three situational factors into consideration including leader-member relations, task structure, and position power.

6. Path-goal theory incorporates both situational and contingency factors in its explanation of leadership.

7. The basic deficiency of leader-participation model is its complexity.

8. Situational Leadership Theory focuses on the ability of the leader to adapt to the context and has little concern for the follower.

9. Charismatic leadership can be seen as a type of trait theory because it is the characteristics the leader demonstrates that make him/her a charismatic leader.

10. Key to visionary leadership is the dual abilities of creating and articulating a vision. You can not have visionary leadership unless both abilities are demonstrated.

11. Transformational and transactional leadership theories are on opposite ends of the same leadership continuum; they are opposing theories.

12. Team leaders have a number of roles and responsibilities. Their most important priority is managing conflict within the team.

13. The importance of leadership depends on the context in which leadership would be exercised.

14. The most fragile, easily damaged form of trust is knowledge-based trust.

15. Identification-based trust differs from other forms of trust in terms of the emotional connection between the individuals.

Answers to Chapter 11 Study Quiz

Multiple Choice (Page - Answer)

1. c-345	6. c-362	11. b-360
2. a-346	7. c-354	12. c-362
3. b-348	8. b-355	13. b-363
4. d-350	9. a-356	14. c-365
5. a-351	10. a-358	15. d-366

True/False

1. T-345	6. T-354	11. F-361
2. T-347	7. T-355	12. F-363
3. F-349	8. F-356	13. T-364
4. F-349	9. T-358	14. F-366
5. T-352	10. T-359	15. T-368

CHAPTER 12 - COMMUNICATION AND INTERPERSONAL SKILLS

LEARNING OUTCOMES
After reading this chapter, students should be able to:
1. Define communication and explain why it is important to managers.
2. Describe the communication process.
3. List techniques for overcoming communication barriers.
4. Identify behaviors related to effective active listening.
5. Explain what behaviors are necessary for providing effective feedback.
6. Describe the contingency factors influencing delegation.
7. Identify behaviors related to effective delegating.
8. Describe the steps in analyzing and resolving conflict.
9. Explain why a manager might stimulate conflict.
10. Contrast distributive and integrative bargaining.

Use the Outline to Guide Your Note Taking from the Text

Considerations as you read
1. When you talk with someone you've never met before, how might you use what you learn about the communication process model to communicate more effectively?
2. How do your nonverbal cues impact your communication with others?
3. Are there any particular communication barriers that impact your communications?
4. How can you overcome those barriers?
5. What are effective interpersonal communication skills?
6. How do you empower others through effective delegation?
7. How do you feel about conflict? How would you decide what to do about conflicts in your work?

I. UNDERSTANDING COMMUNICATION
A. Introduction
1. Everything a manager does involves communicating.
2. A manager
3. Once a decision is made
4. Good communication skills

B. How Does the Communication Process Work?
1. Communication can be thought of as
2. Communication requires
3. Four conditions affect the encoded message
4. One's total communicative success includes
5. Our attitudes
6. We are restricted in our communicative activity by
7. As attitudes influence our behavior
8. The message is
9. Our message is affected by
10. The channel is
11. The receiver is the
12. The message must be translated into
13. The final link in the communication process is

C. Are Written Communications More Effective Than Verbal Ones?
1. Written communications are
2. Written messages have their drawbacks

D. Is the Grapevine an Effective Way to Communicate?
1. The grapevine is
2. Information is spread by word of mouth
3. The biggest question focuses on
4. Research on this topic

E. How Do Nonverbal Cues Affect Communications?
1. Some of the most meaningful communications are
2. Body language refers to
3. Verbal intonation refers to
4. The nonverbal component is

F. Is the Wave of Communication's Future in Electronic Media?
1. E-mail is one
2. But it's also public information, and as such
3. E-mail has taken on

G. What Barriers Exist to Effective Communication
1. A number of interpersonal and intrapersonal barriers effect the decoding of a message
2. Filtering refers to
3. Selective perception
4. Information overload
5. Emotions
6. Language
7. While we speak a common language
8. An estimated 5 to 20 percent of the population
9. Studies demonstrate that oral-communication apprehensives
10. Of greater concern is the evidence that high-oral-communication apprehensives

H. How Can Managers Overcome Communication Barriers?
1. See Exhibit 12-3.
2. Why Use Feedback?
3. Why Should Simplified Language Be Used?
4. Why Must We Listen Actively?
5. Why Must We Constrain Emotions?
6. Why the Emphasis on Nonverbal Cues?

II. INTERNATIONAL INSIGHTS INTO AND GENDER ISSUES IN THE COMMUNICATION PROCESS
A. Do men and women communicate in the same way?
1. The differences may lead to
2. Deborah Tannen found that when men talk
3. Effective communication between the sexes is
4. Interpersonal communication
5. Owing to the emphasis on the individual
6. In collectivist countries such as Japan
7. U.S. organizations emphasize

146

III. DEVELOPING INTERPERSONAL SKILLS

A. The Importance of Interpersonal Skills
1. A survey of 191 top executives
2. The Center for Creative Leadership in North Carolina
3. A comprehensive study of people

B. Why Are Active Listening Skills Important?
1. Listening requires
2. Effective listening is
3. The human brain is capable of
4. There are four essential requirements for active listening
5. Intensity
6. Empathy requires you to put yourself into the speaker's shoes.
7. An active listener demonstrates acceptance.
8. The final ingredient is taking responsibility for completeness.
9. Just how, though, can you develop effective listening skills?

C. Why Are Feedback Skills Important?
1. If the feedback is positive
2. Negative feedback is

D. What Is the Difference between Positive and Negative Feedback?
1. Managers treat positive and negative feedback
2. Positive feedback is
3. Negative feedback
4. You need to be aware of
5. Research indicates that negative feedback is
6. How Do You Give Effective Feedback?

E. What Are Empowerment Skills?
1. Millions of employees and teams of employees are making key operating decisions that directly affect their work.
2. The increased use of empowerment is being driven by two forces.
3. Delegation is
4. Participative decision making
5. Don't managers abdicate their responsibility when they delegate?
6. How much authority should a manager delegate?
7. How do you delegate effectively?

F. How Do You Manage Conflict?
1. The ability to manage conflict is
2. A study revealed that
3. What is conflict management?
4. Over the years, three differing views have evolved toward conflict in organizations.
5. The traditional view
6. The human relations view
7. The most recent perspective
8. Can conflict be positive and negative?
9. How does a manager tell whether a conflict is functional or dysfunctional?
10. If conflict is dysfunctional, what can a manager do?
11. What are the conflict-handling styles?

    12. Which conflicts do you handle?

    13. Who are the conflict players?

    14. What are the sources of the conflict?

    15. How does a manager stimulate conflict?

    16. There is a dearth of ideas on conflict-stimulation techniques.

    17. The following are some preliminary suggestions that managers might want to use.

G. What Are Negotiation Skills?
1. Negotiation is a process
2. To achieve this goal, both parties typically use a bargaining strategy.
3. How do bargaining strategies differ?
4. Distributive bargaining
5. Integrative problem solving
6. We see more integrative bargaining in organizations because

H. How Do You Develop Effective Negotiation Skills?
1. The essence of effective negotiation
2.
3.
4.
5.
6.
7.

I. What is an Effective Presentation?
1. The ability to deliver effective presentations
2. How do you make a presentation?
3. What about delivery issues?

REVIEW QUESTIONS

1. Take a conversation between you and your professor and diagram it according to the communication process model in the text.
   Answer – Pages 377-378

2. When should you use oral communication and written communication in an organization?
   Answer – Pages 378-37

3. What part does nonverbals play in the communication process?
   Answer – Pages 379-380

4. Outline the various barriers to effective communication describing each.
   Answer – Pages 380-382

5. Describe the techniques that managers can use to over come the barriers you've described in number 4 above.
   Answer – Pages 383-385

6. How does gender impact communication?
   Answer – Pages 385-386

7. Describe effective feedback, both negative and positive.
   Answer – Pages 388-390

8. How can a manager effectively empower his/her employees through delegation of responsibilities?
   Answer – Pages 391-393

9. When is conflict helpful in an organization? When is it dysfunctional?
   Answer – Pages 394-395

10. What questions do you need to ask yourself when you are trying to manage a conflict at work?
    Answer – Pages 396-398

11. Describe the steps of an effective negotiation.
    Answer – Pages 401-402

12. How do you conduct an effective presentation?
    Answer – Pages 402-404

STUDY QUIZ
Multiple Choice Questions
1. The communication process begins with:
   a) encoding.
   b) eliminating noise.
   c) selecting a channel.
   d) the communication source.

2. In the communication process model, the element which helps the communicator check how successful the transference of understanding has been is the ____ element.
   a) noise
   b) channel
   c) feedback
   d) encoding

3. The emphasis that someone gives to the words or phrases he/she speaks when communicating with others is known as:
   a) nonverbal language.
   b) verbal intonation.
   c) body language.
   d) jargon.

4. Jen's struggle to keep up with her e-mail and phone messages caused her to not listen to an entire message on her answering service, resulting in her misunderstanding what a customer wanted. This is an example of which communication barrier?
   a) Communication apprehension.
   b) Information overload.
   c) Emotions.
   d) Filtering.

5. If a manager wants to overcome the communication barrier of misunderstanding by checking the accuracy of what was said, he/she should:
    a) use feedback.
    b) constrain his/her emotions.
    c) watch for nonverbal cues.
    d) use jargon.

6. Men and women differ in several ways in their communication, such as:
    a) men use communication to clarify and think out loud.
    b) women communication in order to come to a solution of a problem.
    c) women use communication to build relationships, men to exercise control.
    d) men use communication to express how they are feeling about a situation.

7. The number one reason managers lose their jobs according to a survey of Fortune 500 companies is:
    a) poor communication skills.
    b) an inability to manage conflict.
    c) an unwillingness to adopt new technology.
    d) poor interpersonal skills.

8. "Maya, students are uncomfortable with your interpersonal interaction in your office. You seem distant and defensive when they ask questions. Please work on this." This feedback violates which component of effective feedback?
    a) Focusing on specific behavior.
    b) Directing feedback to behavior that the receiver can control.
    c) Keeping the feedback personal.
    d) It violates all of these.

9. Which of the following is true about delegation as a tool of empowerment?
    a) Delegation is the abdication of a manager's responsibility.
    b) Delegation is synonymous with participation.
    c) Delegation requires the assignment of authority along with responsibility.
    d) Delegation slows the decision process but enhances employee self-esteem.

10. Tom delegated researching a benefit plan for the company to Ben. To delegate this project effectively Tom needs to:
    a) let Ben decide with him the boundaries of his authority.
    b) specify Ben's range of discretion.
    c) establish feedback controls.
    d) do all these things.

11. Jim periodically gives somewhat ambiguous instructions to his project teams, hoping to stimulate some mild conflict in order to create better ideas. Jim's perspective on conflict is probably most compatible with:
    a) the traditional view of conflict.
    b) a dysfunctional view of conflict.
    c) the human relations view of conflict.
    d) an interactionist view of conflict.

12. When faced with a conflict Zena always seeks to win. She is most concerned about getting her needs met, regardless of other's needs. Zena's preferred conflict management style is most likely to be:
    a) accommodating.
    b) collaborating.
    c) compromise.
    d) forcing.

13. Joan's project team is in conflict with Gabriel's. Their problem seems to lie in that Joan and Gabriel are in competition for the most effective team leader reward and therefore will not allow their teams to collaborate when it's appropriate. The source of their conflict seems to be:
    a) personal.
    b) structural.
    c) communication differences.
    d) the lack of sufficient resources.

14. Zoe is in a negotiation over buying a used boat from a neighbor. She is willing to pay between $1500 and $1750 for it. The neighbor is willing to accept between $1700 and $1900 for it. The overlap between Zoe's upper range and the neighbor's lower range is known as:
    a) their mutual resistance point.
    b) Zoe's aspiration range.
    c) the settlement range.
    d) the distribution point.

15. An effective presentation should include:
    a) the use of PowerPoint to support the speaker's points.
    b) an opportunity for listeners to ask questions.
    c) as little evidence as possible, focusing on the concepts of the presentation.
    d) all of these elements.

True/False Questions

1. When we talk about the communication process, we are talking about the transferring and understanding of meaning.

2. When a subordinate reads a memo from his boss and then acts on it, the subordinate is decoding the message his boss has sent him.

3. Generally speaking, the vast majority of the information in the company grapevine is completely accurate.

4. Between 5 and 20 percent of people suffer from communication apprehension.

5. An effective way to overcome one or more of the communication barriers inherent in the communication process is to use jargon.

6. Men and women communicate in the same way and any perceived differences are actually very superficial.

7. Active listening requires the listener to focus on the speaker, to place him/herself in the speaker's place, to resist the message forcing the speaker to be persuasive, and to critically analyze the message.

151

8. Effective feedback is personal, general, and goal-oriented.

9. Delegation is the assignment of authority to another person to carry out specific activities.

10. The first step in effective delegation is to clarify the assignment.

11. The perspective that conflict is good and is necessary to stimulate innovation is the human relations view of conflict.

12. The conflict management strategy that is the lowest in terms of both cooperativeness and assertiveness is compromise.

13. Structure of an organization can be a significant source of conflict in an organization.

14. Being a devil's advocate in an organization is simply the process of bringing two or more parties together to make a joint decision and come to an agreement.

15. Integrative bargaining is a negotiation where at least one potential settlement involves no loss to either party.

Answers to Chapter 12 Study Quiz

Multiple Choice (Page - Answer)

1. d-377	6. c-385	11. d-394
2. c-378	7. d-386	12. d-396
3. b-379	8. a-389	13. a-397
4. b-381	9. c-391	14. c-401
5. a-383	10. d-393	15. b-403

True/False

1. T-377	6. F-385	11. F-394
2. T-378	7. F-387	12. F-396
3. F-379	8. F-389	13. T-397
4. T-382	9. T-391	14. F-399
5. F-384	10. T-392	15. T-401

Part 5 - Controlling
CHAPTER 13 - FOUNDATIONS OF CONTROL

LEARNING OUTCOMES
After reading this chapter you should be able to:
1. Define control.
2. Describe three approaches to control.
3. Explain why control is important.
4. Describe the control process.
5. Distinguish between the three types of control.
6. Describe the qualities of an effective control system.
7. Identify the contingency factors in the control process.
8. Explain how controls can become dysfunctional.
9. Describe how national differences influence the control process.
10. Identify the ethical dilemmas in employee monitoring.

Considerations as you read
1. How do you feel about control? What role does control play in your own life?
2. Why is control important in business?
3. What do you do when there is a gap between what you wanted and what you did? What would you do as a manager if this happened with your employees?
4. What kinds of control are there?
5. Can you describe the qualities of an effective control system?
6. How can controls become dysfunctional?
7. What are the ethical issues inherent in control systems in organizations?

I. WHAT IS CONTROL?
A. Introduction
1. Control is
2. There are generally three different approaches to designing control systems
3. Market control
4. Bureaucratic control
5. Clan control
6. The organization is guided and controlled by
7. An organization typically chooses to

II. THE IMPORTANCE OF CONTROL
A. Introduction
1. There is no assurance
2. Control is the final link
3. The value of control lies mostly in

B. The Control Process
1. Three separate and distinct steps
2. The control process assumes that

C. What Is Measuring?
1. The first step in control.
2. How do managers measure?
3. Four common sources of information

4. What do managers measure?
5. How do managers determine discrepancies between actual performance and planned goals?

D. What Managerial Action Can Be Taken?
1. The third and final step in the control process is taking managerial action.
2. Managers can choose among three courses of action
3. If the source of the variation has been deficient performance
4. It is also possible that the variance was a result of an unrealistic standard

III. TYPES OF CONTROL
A. See Exhibit 13-5.

B. What Is Feedforward Control?
1. The most desirable type of control
2. Feedforward controls allow

C. When Is Concurrent Control Used?
1. It takes place
2. The best-known form of concurrent control is

D. Why Is Feedback Control So Popular?
1. The most popular type of control relies on feedback.
2. The major drawback of this type of control is
3. First, feedback provides managers with
4. Second, feedback control can

IV. QUALITIES OF AN EFFECTIVE CONTROL SYSTEM
A. Common Qualities
1. Accuracy
2. Timeliness
3. Economy
4. Flexibility
5. Understandability
6. Reasonable criteria
7. Strategic placement
8. Emphasis on the exception
9. Multiple criteria
10. Corrective action

V. CONTINGENCY FACTORS OF CONTROL
A. The Validity of Effective Control Systems is Influenced by Situational Factors
1. See Exhibit 13-6.
2. Control systems should vary to reflect the size of the organization
3. The higher one moves in the organization's hierarchy
4. The greater the degree of decentralization
5. The organizational culture may be one of
6. As with leadership styles, motivation techniques,
7. Finally, the importance of an activity influences

VI. ADJUSTING CONTROLS FOR NATIONAL DIFFERENCES
A. What about Organizations that Operate Worldwide?
1. Methods of controlling employee behavior and operations
2. The differences are primarily in
3. Managers of foreign operations of multinational corporations
4. Distance creates a tendency to
5. Technology's impact on control is
6. Constraints on managerial corrective action may

VII. THE DYSFUNCTIONAL SIDE OF CONTROLS
A. Introduction
1. UPS example
2. When controls are inflexible or control standards are unreasonable
3. Problems can occur when
4. Dysfunctionality is caused by
5. To avoid being reprimanded
6. Failure to design flexibility into a control system can

VIII. ETHICAL ISSUES OF CONTROL
A. Difficult Questions
1. Technological advances have made the process of controlling much easier.
2. But these advances have also brought with them ethical questions.
3. Special attention needs to be given to the topic of employee monitoring.
4. Technological advancements
5. Employers can
6. One area of debate over employee workplace privacy is
7. Computer monitoring is another area in which ethical questions arise.
8. How can organizations benefit from the control information provided by computer monitoring systems and yet minimize the potential behavioral and legal drawbacks?
9. Ethical issues associated with control
10. Employer involvement
11. Today, many organizations, in their quest to control safety and health insurance costs,
12. Controlling employees' behaviors
13. Rather, the law is based on the premise that

REVIEW QUESTIONS
1. What are the different forms of control? When is each most effective?
   Answer – Pages 412-414

2. What part does measurement play in the control process?
   Answer – Pages 415-416

3. What can a manager do about discrepancies between actual performance and planned goals?
   Answer – Pages 417-419

4. Describe the various types of control.
   Answer – Pages 420-421

5. Outline the qualities of an effective control system.
   Answer – Pages 421-422

6. Review what part contingency factors play in the control process in an organization.
   Answer – Pages 422-423

7. How can control become dysfunctional?
   Answer – Pages 425-426

8. Discuss what ethical issues are involved in organizational control.
   Answer – Pages 426-428

STUDY QUIZ
Multiple Choice Questions

1. If NTI, a manufacturing company depends on its policies, regulations, standardization of activities, etc., for control, it is using _____ control.
   a) bureaucratic
   b) variation
   c) market
   d) clan

2. Ryan depends on corporate values, traditions, and culture to control employee performance and company innovation. Ryan is using _____ control.
   a) bureaucratic
   b) variation
   c) market
   d) clan

3. The control process is built on one key assumption, which is:
   a) both qualitative and quantitative controls are used in tandem.
   b) that planning precedes control.
   c) standards are inflexible and unchanging.
   d) concurrent control is more effective than feedforward control.

4. There are several ways to measure performance. If you need a method that is formal, comprehensive, concise, and that lend itself to cataloging, your best choice of measurement system is:
   a) personal observation.
   b) oral reports.
   c) written reports.
   d) computer monitoring.

5. In general, organization control systems tend to be directed at:
   a) information.
   b) operations.
   c) finances.
   d) all of these and more.

6. When a manager needs to take correction action to correct deficiencies in performance, he/she has several options, including:
   a) raising standards.
   b) lowering standards.
   c) correcting individual performance.
   d) all of these.

7. The most desirable form of control is:
   a) feedforward.
   b) concurrent.
   c) feedback.
   d) none of these.

8. Effective control systems are characterized by:
   a) economy.
   b) understandability.
   c) timeliness.
   d) all of these.

9. The characteristic of effective control systems that focuses managers on critical events, activities, and operations because managers can't afford the time or cost of controlling everything is:
   a) emphasis on the exception.
   b) reasonable criteria.
   c) strategic placement.
   d) corrective action.

10. Formal controls, high number of controls, and elaborate controls are best implemented in an organization:
    a) small in size, relating to a low level position in the organization, and high decentralization.
    b) that is large, with a threatening culture, a high degree of centralization, and when the activity is important.
    c) when the activity is relatively unimportant, when there is high centralization, and the organization has an open and supportive culture.
    d) that is large, low decentralization, and relatively low level position.

11. The importance of an activity has much to do with its control, as a consequence:
    a) if the control effort is costly and the consequences of problems are small, the control system will not be elaborate.
    b) if the control effort is costly and the consequences of problems are big, the control system will not be elaborate.
    c) if control is relatively inexpensive and the consequences of problems are big, the control system will not be elaborate.
    d) if control is relatively inexpensive and the consequences of problems are small, the control system will be elaborate.

12. In less developed countries, control is often most dependent on:
    a) direct supervision.
    b) written reports.
    c) oral reports.
    d) computer monitoring.

13. In terms of the dysfunctional aspects of control, employee manipulation of control data often depends on:
    a) the opportunity.
    b) the legality of the behavior.
    c) the importance of the activity.
    d) the level of the employee within the organization.

14. When it comes to e-mail at work:
    a) 1st Amendments rights apply; the employer can not read employee e-mail.
    b) computer monitoring is not yet sophisticated enough to monitor the volumes of e-mail.
    c) employers may only monitor and read work-related e-mail written by employees.
    d) over a third of employers monitor employee e-mail.

15. When it comes to monitoring and controlling employee behavior off-the-job:
    a) the law prevents employers from doing anything.
    b) it is on the increase.
    c) few, if any, employers currently give it any attention.
    d) almost all employers monitor and seek to control some aspect of employee off-the-job behavior.

True/False Questions

1. Control is essential for managers to understand how well their work units are performing.

2. Clayton's company relies on external market forces to direct and measure the performance of their company. This is an example of bureaucratic control.

3. Control is the final element of the managerial planning process.

4. The control process begins with managers comparing actual performance against a performance standard.

5. The best first-hand source of feedback information for a manager is the use of computers and feedback software.

6. The range of variation is the acceptable variation from standards of any actual performance or accomplishment of an set of organizational goals.

7. Basic corrective action is the immediate correction of any performance problem.

8. The most popular type of control is concurrent control.

9. Feedback control is the least used, least effective type of control because by the time the information reaches the manager it is often too late to correct the deficiency.

10. Effective control systems use multiple criteria and place their emphasis on the exception to the standards of performance.

11. The smaller the organization, the more informal and personal the control systems.

12. Managers of foreign operations of multinational corporations tend to be more closely controlled by the headquarters office than domestic managers are.

13. Controls can harm organizational performance when managers and employees focus on looking good exclusively on those items that are measured.

14. One way to avoid dysfunction in control systems is to build flexibility into the control system.

15. Computer monitoring is an excellent control mechanism while causing stress and pressure for employees who are monitored.

Answers to Chapter 13 Study Quiz

Multiple Choice (Page - Answer)

1. a-413	6. d-419	11. a-424
2. d-414	7. a-420	12. a-425
3. b-415	8. d-421	13. c-426
4. c-416	9. c-422	14. d-427
5. d-417	10. b-423	15. b-428

True/False

1. T-412	6. T-417	11. T-423
2. F-413	7. F-419	12. F-424
3. T-414	8. F-420	13. T-425
4. F-415	9. F-421	14. T-426
5. F-416	10. T-422	15. T-427

CHAPTER 14 - TECHNOLOGY AND OPERATIONS

LEARNING OUTCOMES
After reading this chapter, you should be able to:
1. Describe the formula for calculating productivity.
2. Explain how technology can improve productivity.
3. Explain how information technology is providing managers with decision support.
4. Describe the advantages of computer-aided design.
5. Identify why management might consider introducing flexible manufacturing systems.
6. Define and describe the three key elements in work process engineering.
7. Describe what is meant by the term supply chain management.
8. Explain what is meant by the term just-in-time inventory systems.
9. Identify the steps in developing a PERT network.

Considerations as you read
1. What part does technology play in increasing organizational productivity?
2. How does technology impact worker obsolescence?
3. In what ways is information technology reshaping the work place?
4. Can you explain how technology assists decision making in organizations?
5. Discuss the various forms of technology enhance production processes.
6. What is the PDCA cycle?
7. Explain work process engineering and how it enhances work in the organization.
8. Describe supply chain management and JIT management.
9. Can you review the various tools and elements of project management?

I. TRANSFORMATION PROCESS
A. Described
1. All organizations produce goods or services through
2. The system takes
3. The transformation process applies to
4. The transformation process is
5. The study and application of this transformation process

II. TECHNOLOGY AND PRODUCTIVITY
A. Introduction
1. In its purest form, technology is
2. The term has become widely used to
3. The common feature is that
4. It is the computerization of equipment and machinery
5. In its simplest form, productivity can be expressed in the following ratio:
   Productivity =
6. The above formula can be applied in its total form or broken down into subcategories.
7. Productivity can also be applied at three different levels
8. Since technology is the means by

III. TECHNOLOGY AND WORKER OBSOLESCENCE
A. Examples
1. Rob Hanc
2. Glenna Cheney
3. Changes in technology have

      4. Work process engineering
      5. Software is

IV. TECHNOLOGY TRANSFER
A. Introduction
      1. Example Globe Silk
      2. Technology transfer is
      3. Those organizations that have technology to transfer
      4. Developing countries
      5. Managers will increasingly seek

V. INFORMATION TECHNOLOGY
A. What Is a Management Information System (MIS)?
      1. There is no universally agreed-upon definition.
      2. We define the term as
      3. In theory, this system can be
      4. A library provides a good analogy.
      5. Organizations today are like well-stocked libraries.

B. What Is Workflow Automation?
      1. In the typical office
      2. The whole process requires
      3. Workflow automation can
      4. Workflow automation begins by
      5. Exhibit 14-1 illustrates

C. How Does Technology Enhance Internal Communications?
      1. Information technology is
      2. One of the most important developments in information technology
      3. Wireless products are

D. In What Ways Does Technology Assist Decision Making?
      1. Information technology is
      2. Expert systems use software programs
      3. Neural networks are
      4. Electronic meetings are
      5. The latest wrinkle in decision support software is
          a) Forecast Pro
          b) Business Insight
          c) Performance Now!
          d) Negotiator Pro

VI. OPERATIONS TECHNOLOGY
A. High-tech Manufacturing is Going Global
      1. Satyan Pitroda believes
      2. By importing technology developed elsewhere
      3. See Exhibit 14-2.

B. How Can Products Be Designed More Efficiently?
  1. Technology continues to
  2. Computer-aided design (CAD)
  3. The best CAD software

C. In What Ways Can Production Processes Be Enhanced?
  1. Technological advances
  2. Traditional steelmaking uses a technology
  3. The Cremona mill uses a revolutionary technology that
  4. What is robotics?
  5. What are flexible manufacturing systems?

D. In What Ways Can Customer Service Be Improved?
  1. Consistent with the quality movement, technology can
  2. Managers are using technology to improve their customer service strategies in three ways

E. How Does Technology Enhance Product Distribution?
  1. Traditional distribution technology relied heavily on
  2. It was not unusual for a product to go through
  3. New technologies are
  4. The two most recent breakthroughs in distribution technology are
  5. Cable television channels
  6. Infomercials are
  7. The latest and potentially most exciting distribution channel is

F. Is Close Good Enough?
  1. Continuous process improvement programs are
  2. Eliminate variations
  3. Uniformity
  4. Continuous improvement runs counter to
  5. The search for never-ending improvement requires

G. How Can Process Engineering Enhance Work Processes?
  1. It is considering how things would be done if you could start all over from scratch.
     a) The term comes from
     b) Michael Hammer brought this concept to light.
  2. What are the key elements of work process engineering?
  3. An organization's distinctive competencies are
  4. Management also needs to assess the core processes that
  5. Work process engineering requires
  6. Why work process engineering now?

VII. CURRENT ISSUES IN OPERATIONS
  A. What is Supply Chain Management?
  1. Supply chain management refers to
  2. It focuses on
  3. One of the ways to promote this effort is to
  4. A variation involves

B. What Is a Just-in-Time Inventory Practice?
1. Anything management can do to
2. JIT inventory systems
3. With JIT inventory items arrive
4. The goal of JIT is
5. In Japan, JIT systems are called kanban.
6. An illustration of how JIT works in the U.S. can be seen in
7. The ultimate goal of a JIT inventory system is to

C. Are Continuous Improvement and Quality Control the Same Thing?
1. Continuous improvement is
2. Continuous improvement programs
3. Quality control refers to
4. Quality control will probably
5. Managers need to ask

VIII. PROJECT MANAGEMENT AND CONTROL TOOLS
A. What is Project Management?
1. A project is
2. Project management is
3. Project management has
4. It fits well with
5. In the typical project

B. What is The Role of the Project Manager?
1. The one-shot nature of the work makes project managers
2. The job has to be
3. The role of project manager

C. What Are Some Popular Scheduling Tools?
1. Managers regularly detail
2. How do you use a Gantt chart?
3. A modified version of the Gantt chart is called a load chart.
4. What is a PERT network analysis?
5. What are the key components of PERT?
6. Application of PERT to a construction manager's task of building a 5,500 square foot custom home.
   a) Exhibit 14-8 outlines the major events.
   b) Exhibit 14-9 depicts the PERT network based on the data in Exhibit 14-8.
   c) Slack time is
7. How is PERT both a planning and a control tool?

REVIEW QUESTIONS
1. What is technology transfer and what are the issues related to it?
   Answer – Page 442

2. Explain workflow automation and its impact on organizations.
   Answer – Pages 443-444

3. Describe the various uses of technology to assist organizational and managerial decision making.
   Answer – Pages 445-447

4. How does operations technology enhance work productions?
   Answer – Pages 448-450

5. In what ways can operations technology improve customer service and product distribution?
   Answer – Pages 450-452

6. What is process engineering?
   Answer – Pages 453-454

7. Explain how supply chain management and just-in-time systems improve productivity.
   Answer – Pages 455-456

8. Outline the project management process and the role of the project manager.
   Answer – Pages 457-457

9. Chart the various types of project management tools explain the use of each.
   Answer – Pages 459-463

STUDY QUIZ
Multiple Choice Questions

1. The application of the process through which an organization creates values, turning inputs into outputs is:
   a) service management.
   b) workflow automation.
   c) operations management.
   d) technology transfer.

2. Technology will have a number of impacts on workers in the future including:
   a) changing the worklife of hourly workers but having little impact on professionals.
   b) decreasing the level of education and skill future workers will need on-the-job.
   c) nearly eliminating all types of repetitive tasks.
   d) all of the above.

3. _____ is a system for providing management with necessary information on a regular basis in the form most useful to them.
   a) Management information system
   b) Operations management
   c) Transformation process
   d) Workflow automation

4. Ritter is working on a process to enhance the way documents are created and moved from one manager to another through the use of technology. This is known as:
   a) operations management.
   b) workflow automation.
   c) information management.
   d) a neural network.

5. If Jack is working with computer software that imitates the structure of brain cells in its sophistication, helping robotics make "decisions," then Jack is working on:
   a) a neural network.
   b) workflow automation.
   c) information management.
   d) computer-aided design.

6. _____ is computer software is used to show the geometry of a product by graphically displaying and permitting manipulation of it on a video monitor.
   a) A neural network
   b) Flexible manufacturing design
   c) Robotics
   d) Computer-aided design

7. A bicycle company allows customers to order their bikes customer made over the Internet. They fill in a form that describes their physique and riding habits, preferences as to colors and components. The maker then inputs commands into his computer guided manufacturing system. This permits the mass production of custom-designed bikes. This is an example of:
   a) Workflow automation.
   b) Flexible manufacturing design.
   c) Robotics.
   d) Computer-aided design.

8. Technology can improve customer service in a number of ways, such as:
   a) by personalizing the service.
   b) providing additional support related to product acquisition.
   c) fundamentally transforming their business.
   d) all of these.

9. If a manager is examining the processes within an organization to discover what degree of value each adds to its products, the manager is conducting.
   a) process value analysis.
   b) supply chain management.
   c) workflow automation.
   d) flexible manufacturing design.

10. When managers set up an inventory system that orders and uses components as they arrive rather than ordering ahead and storing the components they are using:
    a) supply chain management.
    b) just-in-time inventory management.
    c) total quality management.
    d) project management.

11. Tammy is working on getting her design team's new product design to the executive management team by their deadline within the parameters the executives set. Tammy's effort is an example of:
    a) supply chain management.
    b) program evaluation and review.
    c) the use of groupware.
    d) project management.

12. Which of the following is true about the role of a project manager?
    a) Sophisticated decision technology has made the role of a project manager obsolete.
    b) It is becoming less popular as companies implement more TQM and employee empowerment programs.
    c) It remains difficult despite the various tools and technologies designed to assist the project manager.
    d) All of these are true.

13. A _____ is a planning tool that allows managers to use bar graphs to track when tasks are supposed to be accomplished and compare proposed deadlines to actual progress.
    a) project management
    b) Gantt chart
    c) PERT chart
    d) load chart

14. When a manager has a large project with a number of activities or projects or that is particularly complex a _____ is a particularly useful management tool.
    a) project management
    b) Gantt chart
    c) Pert chart
    d) load chart

15. In terms of a PERT chart the _____ is the longest or most time-consuming sequence of events and activities required to complete the project in the shortest amount of time.
    a) value process
    b) slack time
    c) load path
    d) critical path

True/False Questions
1. A service organization produces nonphysical outputs.

2. Productivity may be calculated by dividing the outputs of an organization by the number of employees producing the outputs.

3. Software is having almost as much of an impact on the jobs of professionals as it is on the work lives of hourly workers.

4. When knowledge is helpful in improving the production of products or services moves from one country to another you have a transfer of technology.

5. Data is any information that has been analyzed and processed for use by managers.

6. Workflow automation is software designed to help managers analyze and solve ill-structured problems.

7. Groupware is software, more sophisticated than expert systems, that is designed to help managers make decisions and manage projects.

8. The use of robotics is in decline as flexible manufacturing and computer-aided design reduces the need for robots.

9. Flexible manufacturing systems involves the integration of CAD, engineering, and manufacturing.

10. Process engineering involves managers in working with organization's distinctive competencies, assessing core processes, and structural reorganization.

11. Supply chain management involves the management, functions, and activities involved in producing and delivering products or services to customers.

12. Project management is less effective in a dynamic and changing business environment.

13. A load chart is a helpful tool for managers managing complex tasks and multiple projects.

14. In a program evaluation and review activities are those actions that need to take place to accomplish the project.

15. The critical path is the time difference between the critical path and all other paths.

Answers to Chapter 14 Study Quiz

Multiple Choice (Page - Answer)

1. c-439	6. d-448	11. d-457
2. c-441	7. b-450	12. c-458
3. a-443	8. d-451	13. b-459
4. b-444	9. a-454	14. c-460
5. a-446	10. b-456	15. d-462

True/False

1. T-439	6. F-446	11. T-455
2. F-440	7. F-447	12. F-458
3. T-441	8. F-449	13. F-460
4. T-442	9. T-450	14. T-462
5. F-442	10. T-453	15. T-463